ISBN: 9798861623605

"How to enable your children to become financially independent before they turn 45 years old."

By Stock Owl

I0409450

September 2023

Unlock Financial Independence for You and Your Children!

In "How to enable your children to become financially independent before they turn 45 years old," acclaimed author Stock-Owl takes you on a transformative journey through the intricate world of finance, offering invaluable insights into achieving financial independence and paving the way for your children's financial freedom.

Discover the power of asset allocation, the magic of compound interest, and the principles of value investing — all presented in an accessible and engaging manner. This comprehensive guide empowers parents to become effective financial mentors and equips children with the essential tools for a secure financial future.

Learn to navigate budgeting, savings, and investments effectively, and explore real-life success stories that prove the efficacy of astute asset allocation. "How to enable your children to become financially independent before they turn 45 years old" is your roadmap to financial empowerment and a lasting financial legacy.

Embark on this journey to secure your own financial future while nurturing the financial well-being of your children. Whether you're new to finance or a seasoned investor, this book provides actionable strategies that will benefit you and your family for generations to come.

Invest in your financial future today!
Stock-Owl

Table of Contents

Introduction

- Summarizing Key Takeaways
- Encouraging Implementation of How to enable your children to become financially independent before they turn 45 years old

Appendices

- Additional Resources for Financial Education
- Glossary of Financial Terms
- Worksheets and Templates

Acknowledgments

- Recognizing Those Who Supported Your Journey

Index

- Quick Reference Guide to Key Concepts

About the Author

- Learn More About Stock-Owl and Their Expertise

Introduction: Welcome to "How to enable your children to become financially independent before they turn 45 years old"

Welcome to "How to enable your children to become financially independent before they turn 45 years old," a comprehensive guide on how to empower your children to achieve financial independence well before they reach the age of 45. If you're reading this, you've taken the first step toward securing your children's financial future, and I commend you for your commitment to their success.

Setting the Stage for Financial Independence

Picture this: your children, in their early forties, enjoying a life free from financial worries, pursuing their passions, and making choices based on their dreams, not their bank account balances. This isn't a pipe dream; it's a tangible goal that can be achieved with the right knowledge, strategy, and dedication.

As Stock-Owl, a specialist in value investing, I've had the privilege of helping countless individuals and families build their wealth through smart financial decisions. Now, I'm excited to share with you "How to enable your children to become financially independent before they turn 45 years old," a roadmap that will guide you in nurturing your children's financial independence.

In the pages that follow, we will embark on a journey that covers every aspect of financial education and asset allocation. Whether you're completely new to the world of finance or have some experience, this book is designed to be accessible and practical. You don't need a degree in economics or a background in investing to understand and apply the principles outlined here.

We will start by demystifying the concept of money and explaining the role it plays in our lives. We'll explore the power of compounding, a force that, when harnessed through proper asset allocation, can work wonders over time. I will also underscore your role as a financial mentor to your children and why teaching them about money and asset allocation is of paramount importance.

Building upon this foundation, we'll delve into practical steps for setting up investment accounts, creating a wealth growth strategy, and teaching financial discipline. You'll learn not only what to do but also how to do it effectively.

We will explore success stories of families who have successfully followed How to enable your children to become financially independent before they turn 45 years old and examine the challenges they overcame along the way. Additionally, we'll discuss strategies for preparing your children for financial responsibility and the importance of responsible asset management, even in the context of inheritance.

By the time you finish reading this book, you'll have a clear roadmap for empowering your children to take control of their financial destinies. You'll be armed with the knowledge and tools to guide them on a path to financial independence, setting them up for a life of opportunity, security, and fulfillment.

So, let's begin this journey together and lay the groundwork for your children's financial success. Turn the page, and let's get started on "How to enable your children to become financially independent before they turn 45 years old."

Part I: Laying the Foundation

Chapter 1: Understanding Money

Money, in its essence, is the lifeblood of our financial existence. It serves as a catalyst that propels us through the journey of life, facilitating our desires, dreams, and aspirations. In this chapter, we will embark on a comprehensive exploration of money — its multifaceted role, its significance in our lives, and why the deliberate allocation of money for assets stands as a critical financial cornerstone.

The Role of Money in Our Lives

Imagine, for a moment, a world without money — a world where we must rely on the cumbersome barter system, swapping goods and services directly. While this may seem like an intriguing thought experiment, it's far from practical in our complex, modern society. Money, in its various forms, serves as a lubricant for the wheels of commerce and human interaction. Here, we'll uncover the multifarious roles it plays:

- **Money as a Means of Exchange:** At its core, money simplifies the process of trade. It enables us to conduct transactions smoothly, allowing the exchange of goods and services without the complications of bartering. Consider the convenience of buying groceries, paying rent, or acquiring your morning coffee — all made possible by money.

- **Money as a Store of Value:** Beyond its role in daily transactions, money assumes the role of a store of value. It empowers us to preserve and accumulate wealth over time. Whether in the form of savings accounts, investments, or physical assets, money allows us to safeguard our financial well-being.

- **Money as a Unit of Account:** Money serves as a universal measure of value. It provides a common yardstick by which we can compare the worth of various items, assets, or services. This standardization simplifies decision-making processes and ensures clarity in financial dealings.

- **Money as a Standard of Deferred Payment:** The concept of credit and loans hinges on money's ability to act as a standard of deferred payment. It facilitates transactions where payments are made at a future date. Mortgages, car loans, and installment plans are prime examples.

However, it's essential to recognize that money is not static; its value can fluctuate over time due to factors like inflation or economic changes. This dynamic nature underscores the importance of prudent financial management—particularly, the strategic allocation of money for assets.

The Priority of Allocating Money for Assets

Herein lies a central tenet of financial wisdom: allocate money for assets before addressing liabilities. This principle, often overlooked but critically important, is the bedrock of financial independence. Let's dissect this fundamental concept:

Assets represent investments or possessions with the potential to generate income and appreciate in value over time. These might encompass a diverse array of options, such as stocks, real estate, bonds, or even entrepreneurial ventures.

Liabilities, on the other hand, manifest as financial obligations or debts requiring regular payments. This category encompasses mortgages, loans, credit card debts, and everyday expenses.

The crux of this principle is simple yet profound: by allocating a portion of your income toward the acquisition and cultivation of assets, you effectively create a fertile ground for the seeds of wealth to grow. Rather than channeling all your resources into servicing liabilities and covering daily expenses, diverting a fraction towards investments holds the potential for your wealth to burgeon through the magic of compounding.

In essence, asset allocation is akin to sowing seeds in fertile soil; it's about prioritizing long-term financial growth and security by putting your money to work for you. As we navigate the chapters ahead, you'll not only comprehend the significance of this principle but also gain the practical insights and tools necessary to implement it effectively — setting the stage for your children's financial independence.

In the ensuing chapters, we'll embark on a journey to explore the concept of compounding, your pivotal role as a financial mentor, and a plethora of pragmatic strategies aimed at constructing a robust financial foundation for your family. Together, we'll continue on this enlightening path toward financial empowerment and the assurance of a secure future.

Chapter 2: The Power of Compounding

In the world of finance, few concepts possess the transformative potential of compounding. It is akin to a silent but mighty force that has the ability to turn small investments into substantial wealth over time. This chapter is dedicated to unraveling the intricacies of compounding—how it operates, its astounding impact, and how it can be further elevated when strategically intertwined with the art of asset allocation.

How Compounding Works

Compounding is a phenomenon that can be likened to a financial miracle, operating with astonishing subtlety yet yielding remarkable results. At its core, it is the process by which an initial sum of money, your principal, generates earnings or interest. Crucially, these earnings, in turn, generate more earnings. This cycle repeats and intensifies, leading to exponential growth. Let's delve deeper into its mechanics:

To illustrate, imagine you invest $1,000 into an instrument offering an annual return of 10%. In the initial year, your investment yields $100 in earnings, bringing your total to $1,100. However, the magic of compounding lies in what happens next. During the second year, your 10% return is not merely calculated on your initial $1,000; it encompasses the entire $1,100. Consequently, your earnings for the second year amount to $110, not just $100. This elevates your total to $1,210.

This compounding cycle perpetuates, with your investment generating returns on both the principal amount and the accumulated earnings from previous years. Over time, the effect snowballs, leading to substantial wealth accumulation. In essence, it's akin to a financial snowball rolling downhill, gathering size and momentum as it progresses.

The key insight is that the longer your money remains subjected to the compounding process, the more potent its effects become. This is why early investments often yield the most significant returns and form a foundational principle in the journey toward financial independence.

Amplifying Growth through Asset Allocation

Now, let's pivot to the enthralling interplay between compounding and asset allocation—a strategy that elevates the potential for growth to unprecedented levels. While compounding possesses intrinsic power, this power is magnified when aligned with astute asset allocation.

Recall our earlier discussion regarding the importance of allocating money for assets before addressing liabilities. The brilliance of this approach becomes evident when we explore the synergy between compounding and assets. Here's the synergy in action:

Suppose you commit $10,000 to a diversified portfolio of stocks known for an average annual return of 8%. As we've witnessed, your initial investment undergoes growth through the compounding process. Yet, the real magic is in what transpires as your assets generate income — dividends from stocks, rental income from real estate, or interest from bonds. These earnings become integral components of the compounded growth trajectory.

Over time, the compounding effect on your assets transforms into a torrential stream of wealth accumulation. Your portfolio flourishes not solely through capital appreciation but also via the reinvestment of income generated by those assets. This synergy is the cornerstone in the construction of financial independence, as it permits your wealth to flourish autonomously, necessitating minimal intervention.

In this chapter, we've embarked on an exploration of the marvel of compounding and its potential for transformation. However, the true magic materializes when compounding is harnessed synergistically with the precision of strategic asset allocation. In the chapters that follow, we will venture deeper into the mechanics of asset allocation, arming you with the essential tools and insights required to master this potent combination. As we continue on this enriching journey, you will be primed to unlock the full potential of your financial future.

Chapter 3: Your Role as a Financial Mentor

In the grand tapestry of life, few responsibilities are as profound and far-reaching as that of a parent. It's a role filled with love, care, and the ceaseless pursuit of a brighter future for your children. As you embrace the journey of enabling your children to become financially independent, one of your paramount roles is that of a financial mentor. In this chapter, we will explore the multifaceted dimensions of this role, emphasizing the critical importance of parental involvement in financial education and the art of teaching asset allocation to the next generation.

Parental Responsibility in Financial Education

When it comes to nurturing your children's financial acumen, your influence as a parent is unparalleled. Financial education isn't merely an extracurricular endeavor; it's an essential life skill that will empower your children to navigate the complexities of the financial world with confidence and competence. Here, we underscore the following key aspects of your responsibility:

1. Leading by Example: Children are observant and often mimic the behaviors of their parents. Therefore, your own financial habits and attitudes towards money serve as an implicit lesson. Demonstrating prudent financial practices, such as budgeting, saving, and responsible investing, can instill invaluable lessons in your children.

Your role as a financial mentor begins with your own financial conduct. It's crucial to lead by example. Children often absorb financial behaviors and attitudes from their parents, consciously or subconsciously. Thus, your financial habits, whether frugal or extravagant, diligent or haphazard, will leave a lasting impression on your children. Demonstrating prudent financial practices lays a solid foundation for their own financial education.

2. Fostering Open Communication: An environment of open and non-judgmental communication is fundamental to effective financial education. Encourage your children to ask questions, share their financial concerns, and seek guidance when needed. This open dialogue will cultivate a healthy attitude toward money.

Healthy communication is the linchpin of effective financial education. Create an environment where your children feel comfortable discussing money matters without fear of judgment. Encourage them to ask questions, express their financial concerns, and seek guidance when necessary. In doing so, you foster a culture of open dialogue that will serve as a bedrock for their financial understanding.

3. Age-Appropriate Lessons: Tailor your financial lessons to the developmental stage of your children. Younger children might start with basic concepts of money, while teenagers can delve into more advanced topics like investing and asset allocation.

The age and developmental stage of your children should dictate the complexity of your financial lessons. For younger children, simple concepts like saving, spending, and basic budgeting can be introduced through real-world examples like allowances. As your children grow older, gradually introduce them to more advanced financial topics, such as investing, compound interest, and asset allocation, adapting the lessons to their evolving comprehension.

4. Setting Financial Goals: Teach your children the importance of setting financial goals. Whether it's saving for a special toy or planning for college, instilling the habit of goal-setting helps them develop a sense of purpose and responsibility.

Instill in your children the value of setting financial goals. These goals need not be grandiose; they can be as simple as saving for a favorite toy or a special outing. Setting and achieving financial goals imparts a sense of purpose and responsibility, reinforcing the idea that money can be a tool to achieve their dreams.

5. Practical Money Management: As your children grow, involve them in practical money management. Allowances, budgeting exercises, and savings accounts can be invaluable tools to teach financial responsibility.

Practical money management is a crucial aspect of their financial education. Consider giving your children allowances, helping them create budgets, and opening savings accounts in their names. These hands-on experiences provide a real-world understanding of money management, where they can apply the concepts they've learned.

6. Learning from Mistakes: Financial mistakes are inevitable, even for adults. Emphasize that mistakes are opportunities for learning. Encourage your children to analyze what went wrong and how they can make better financial decisions in the future.

Mistakes are an inherent part of financial education. Just as adults make financial blunders, your children will too. The key is to frame these mistakes as opportunities for learning and growth. Encourage your children to reflect on what went wrong, why it happened, and how they can make wiser financial choices in the future. This process instills resilience and a growth mindset toward financial matters.

Teaching Asset Allocation to Children

Asset allocation, although perceived as a complex financial concept, can be introduced to children in a simplified manner. Asset allocation is, essentially, the strategic distribution of investments across various asset classes, such as stocks, bonds, and cash equivalents, to optimize returns while managing risk. Here's how you can convey this concept to your children:

1. Introduction to Assets: Begin by explaining what assets are. Assets are things you own that can potentially generate money. Give examples such as stocks, real estate, a business, or even a savings account.

Start by introducing the concept of assets. Explain that assets are things you own that have the potential to generate money. Provide concrete examples like owning shares of a company (stocks), owning a house or apartment (real estate), having your own business, or even keeping money in a bank account (savings account). This tangible introduction helps demystify the term "assets."

2. The Piggy Bank Analogy: A simple analogy is comparing asset allocation to a piggy bank. Imagine you have three piggy banks: one for saving, one for spending, and one for investing. You can allocate your allowance or earnings into these three piggy banks. The saving piggy bank ensures you have money for the future, the spending piggy bank is for everyday expenses, and the investing piggy bank helps your money grow over time.

To explain asset allocation, use a relatable analogy — a piggy bank. Envision three piggy banks, each serving a distinct purpose: saving, spending, and investing. The saving piggy bank safeguards money for the future, the spending piggy bank covers everyday expenses, and the investing piggy bank is where money grows over time. This simple visualization helps children grasp the idea that money can have different purposes and growth potential.

3. Diversification: Teach the importance of not putting all their money in one piggy bank. Explain that just like a farmer plants different crops to reduce the risk of losing everything if one crop fails, diversifying their piggy banks by allocating money into different assets can reduce financial risk.

Introduce the concept of diversification, a fundamental principle of asset allocation. Compare it to a farmer planting various crops to minimize the risk of losing everything if one crop fails. Explain that, similarly, spreading their money across different piggy banks — representing various assets — can reduce the risk of financial loss. This helps children understand the importance of not putting all their resources into a single investment or asset.

4. The Long-Term Vision: Encourage a long-term perspective. Explain that some piggy banks, like the investing one, are for long-term goals like buying a car or a house, or even retiring comfortably. This introduces the idea that money can work for them over time.

Instill a long-term perspective by emphasizing that certain piggy banks, such as the investing one, are for long-term goals. Explain that these goals could include buying a car, purchasing a house, or even retiring comfortably someday. This introduces the concept that money can be a tool that works for them over time, helping them achieve their aspirations.

5. Regular Review: Periodically review the contents of each piggy bank with your children. Discuss how much money is in each and whether it's allocated according to their financial goals. This practice instills discipline and responsibility.

Implement a routine of reviewing the contents of each piggy bank with your children. Sit down together and assess how much money is in each piggy bank and whether the allocation aligns with their financial goals. This regular review instills discipline and responsibility in managing their assets.

Incorporating asset allocation into your children's financial education equips them with a fundamental skill for building and preserving wealth. It encourages a mindset of purposeful money management rather than haphazard spending. As your children grasp the concept of asset allocation, they'll gain a valuable tool for making informed financial decisions and achieving their long-term financial objectives.

In conclusion, your role as a financial mentor to your children is a profound and enduring one. It involves leading by example, fostering open communication, and imparting age-appropriate financial lessons. Teaching asset allocation, even in simplified terms, can set the stage for a lifetime of financial wisdom. As we progress through this book, we'll continue to expand on these principles and explore how they integrate with our overarching goal of enabling your children to become financially independent. Your commitment to their financial education is an investment in their future prosperity, and it's a journey well worth undertaking.

Part II: Building Financial Stability

Chapter 4: Building a Strong Financial Foundation

The journey towards financial independence is akin to constructing a sturdy building. Before erecting the towering structure of wealth, it's essential to lay a strong foundation. In this section, we delve into the pivotal aspects of building this financial bedrock. The cornerstone of this foundation is the practice of budgeting and saving, followed by the strategic allocation of income to savings and investments.

Budgeting and Saving Techniques

Budgeting and saving are the bedrock of financial stability. They are the tools that allow you to manage your finances effectively and ensure that you have the resources to invest and grow your wealth. Let's explore some essential techniques to master these foundational skills:

1. Creating a Budget: Start by creating a comprehensive budget that outlines your income and expenses. This budget serves as your financial roadmap, helping you understand where your money is coming from and where it's going. There are various budgeting methods, such as the 50/30/20 rule (50% for needs, 30% for wants, 20% for savings and debt repayment) or zero-based budgeting (where every dollar has a purpose). Choose a method that suits your family's financial goals and lifestyle.

A budget is not merely a tool for tracking expenses; it's a strategic blueprint for your financial life. It's your financial GPS, helping you chart a course toward your goals. There are several budgeting approaches to consider:

- **The 50/30/20 Rule:** This popular budgeting method suggests allocating 50% of your income to needs (essentials like housing, groceries, and utilities), 30% to wants (non-essentials like dining out and entertainment), and 20% to savings and debt repayment.

- **Zero-Based Budgeting:** With this method, you allocate every dollar of your income to a specific purpose, ensuring that your income minus expenses equals zero. It forces you to give every dollar a job, whether it's for savings, bills, or discretionary spending.

- **Envelope System:** This physical approach involves dividing your cash into envelopes designated for specific categories, like groceries or entertainment. When an envelope is empty, you can't spend more in that category until the next budgeting period.

The budgeting method you choose should align with your financial goals and lifestyle. The key is to create a plan that provides clarity and control over your finances.

2. Tracking Expenses: To gain a clear understanding of your spending habits, diligently track all your expenses. This includes not only major bills but also daily purchases like coffee or snacks. Several apps and online tools can simplify expense tracking, making it easier to identify areas where you can cut back.

Expense tracking is like shining a spotlight on your financial behavior. It reveals patterns, identifies areas of overspending, and highlights opportunities for savings. To effectively track expenses:

- **Use Digital Tools:** There are numerous apps and online platforms that automatically categorize your expenses, providing insights into your spending habits. Popular choices include Mint, YNAB (You Need A Budget), and Personal Capital.

- **Review Statements:** Regularly review your bank and credit card statements. This manual check can help you spot unauthorized transactions and identify any discrepancies or unusual spending.

- **Keep Receipts:** Save receipts for cash purchases and enter them into your expense tracking system. This ensures you capture all expenditures, even those made with physical currency.

Expense tracking is an ongoing process that requires diligence. The more accurately and consistently you track your spending, the better equipped you are to make informed financial decisions.

3. Setting Realistic Goals: Establish clear financial goals for your family. These goals could range from creating an emergency fund to saving for education expenses or retirement. Ensure that your goals are specific, measurable, achievable, relevant, and time-bound (SMART).

Financial goals serve as the compass guiding your financial journey. They provide direction and purpose to your financial decisions. When setting goals:

- **Be Specific:** Clearly define what you want to achieve. For example, instead of a vague goal like "save for retirement," specify "save $1 million for retirement by age 65."

- **Make Them Measurable:** Attach specific numbers or metrics to your goals. This enables you to track progress and know when you've achieved them.

- **Ensure They're Achievable:** Goals should be realistic and attainable within your financial capacity. Setting unattainable goals can lead to frustration and discouragement.

- **Relevance Matters:** Goals should align with your values and priorities. They should be meaningful and resonate with your family's unique circumstances.

- **Set Deadlines:** Establish deadlines for your goals to create a sense of urgency. A timeframe provides structure and motivation.

Common financial goals include:

- **Emergency Fund:** Accumulate three to six months' worth of living expenses in an easily accessible account to cover unexpected events like medical emergencies or job loss.

- **Debt Repayment:** Create a plan to pay off high-interest debts, such as credit card balances or student loans.

- **Education Savings:** Save for your children's education expenses, whether it's for college, vocational training, or other educational pursuits.

- **Retirement:** Develop a retirement savings strategy to ensure financial security during your golden years.

- **Homeownership:** Save for a down payment on a home or invest in real estate.

When you set SMART goals, you transform abstract desires into concrete plans. These plans become the driving force behind your financial decisions, motivating you to stay on track.

4. Paying Yourself First: Treat your savings as a non-negotiable expense in your budget. Before paying bills or spending on non-essential items, allocate a portion of your income to savings. This practice ensures that you prioritize your financial future.

"Paying yourself first" is a fundamental financial principle that prioritizes savings. It means treating your savings as a non-negotiable expense, similar to paying your rent or mortgage. When you receive your income, allocate a portion directly to your savings or investment accounts before spending on other obligations or discretionary purchases.

This approach has several advantages:

- **Consistency:** Paying yourself first establishes a regular savings habit, ensuring that you consistently set aside money for your financial goals.

- **Priority:** It emphasizes the importance of your financial future, making savings a top priority rather than an afterthought.

- **Protection:** By setting aside funds before discretionary spending, you safeguard your financial goals from impulse purchases or unforeseen expenses.

- **Growth:** Consistent contributions to savings or investments enable your money to grow over time through compound interest or investment returns.

To implement "paying yourself first":

- **Automate Savings:** Set up automatic transfers from your checking account to your savings or investment accounts. Automation ensures that savings occur without effort or temptation to spend.

- **Allocate a Percentage:** Determine a specific percentage of your income to allocate to savings. This can be 20%, 10%, or any amount that aligns with your financial goals.

- **Review and Adjust:** Periodically review your savings contributions and adjust them as your financial situation evolves. If your income increases, consider increasing your savings rate as well.

"Paying yourself first" is a powerful practice that transforms savings from a mere intention into a tangible reality. It's a key driver in building financial stability and achieving your financial goals.

5. Emergency Fund: Building an emergency fund is a crucial component of financial stability. Aim to save at least three to six months' worth of living expenses in an easily accessible account. This fund provides a safety net in case of unexpected events like medical emergencies or job loss.

An emergency fund is your financial safety net. It provides a cushion to protect you and your family from unexpected financial setbacks. Whether it's a medical emergency, car repair, or sudden job loss, having an emergency fund ensures that you can cover essential expenses without resorting to high-interest debt.

Consider the following guidelines when establishing and maintaining your emergency fund:

- **Set a Target:** Aim to save at least three to six months' worth of living expenses. This amount provides a substantial safety net without being overly conservative.

- **Accessibility:** Your emergency fund should be easily accessible when needed. High-yield savings accounts, money market accounts, or a separate checking account can serve this purpose.

- **Separate Account:** Consider keeping your emergency fund in a separate account from your everyday spending account. This separation helps prevent accidental spending.

- **Regular Contributions:** Make consistent contributions to your emergency fund until you reach your target. Automate transfers to ensure steady progress.

- **Replenishment:** If you need to dip into your emergency fund for a legitimate emergency, prioritize replenishing it as soon as possible.

An emergency fund offers peace of mind and financial resilience. It allows you to navigate unexpected challenges without derailing your long-term financial goals.

6. Automating Savings: Consider automating your savings by setting up regular transfers from your checking account to your savings or investment accounts. This "pay yourself first" approach removes the temptation to spend money before saving.

Automation is a powerful tool to streamline your financial life and ensure consistent savings. By automating savings, you make it effortless to prioritize your financial goals. Here's how to make the most of automation:

- **Set Up Transfers:** Contact your bank or financial institution to set up recurring transfers from your checking account to your savings or investment accounts. Specify the amount and frequency (e.g., monthly or bi-weekly).

- **Allocate Specific Goals:** If you have multiple financial goals (e.g., emergency fund, retirement savings, and education fund), allocate funds to each goal accordingly. Automation allows you to segment your savings effortlessly.

- **Sync with Paychecks:** Align automated transfers with your income schedule. Consider transferring funds shortly after receiving your paycheck to ensure that savings take precedence.

- **Regular Review:** Periodically review your automated savings plan to ensure it aligns with your current financial goals and capacity. Adjust contributions as needed.

Automation simplifies the savings process and reduces the likelihood of neglecting your financial goals. It transforms savings from an active decision into a passive habit.

7. Cutting Unnecessary Expenses: Regularly review your expenses and identify areas where you can cut costs. This might involve renegotiating utility bills, eliminating unused subscriptions, or reducing discretionary spending.

Reducing unnecessary expenses is a proactive way to free up funds for savings and investments. Over time, small adjustments can yield substantial savings. Here are strategies to trim your expenses:

- **Review Recurring Bills:** Examine recurring expenses like cable TV, internet, and insurance premiums. Can you find more cost-effective plans or negotiate lower rates with providers?

- **Eliminate Unused Subscriptions:** Cancel subscriptions or memberships that you no longer use or derive value from. This includes streaming services, gym memberships, or magazine subscriptions.

- **Meal Planning:** Plan meals, create shopping lists, and cook at home more often. Eating out and ordering takeout can significantly impact your budget.

- **Shop Smart:** Look for sales, use coupons, and buy generic brands when possible. Compare prices before making significant purchases.

- **Reduce Energy Consumption:** Implement energy-saving practices at home, such as adjusting thermostats, using energy-efficient appliances, and sealing drafts.

- **Limit Impulse Purchases:** Delay non-essential purchases by at least 24 hours to evaluate their necessity. Impulse buys can accumulate quickly.

- **Transportation:** Explore cost-effective transportation options, such as carpooling, public transit, or biking, to reduce fuel and maintenance expenses.

- **Entertainment:** Seek low-cost or free entertainment options, such as local events, parks, or free community activities.

Regularly reviewing and optimizing your expenses can free up funds that can be channeled toward your financial goals. It's a proactive approach to maximizing your savings potential.

Allocating Income to Savings and Investments

With budgeting and saving as a firm foundation, the next step is to allocate your income strategically. This allocation involves directing your financial resources towards savings and investments to fuel your family's long-term financial goals. Here's how to approach this critical aspect:

1. Prioritize Savings: Begin by ensuring that you allocate a portion of your income to savings, as highlighted in your budget. This should cover your emergency fund, short-term savings goals (like vacations or home improvements), and long-term goals (such as retirement or your children's education).

Savings should be an integral part of your financial plan, and allocating a portion of your income to savings is the first step in ensuring its priority. Let's explore how you can prioritize savings:

- **Emergency Fund:** Ensure that your emergency fund is adequately funded to cover essential expenses in case of unexpected events.

- **Short-Term Goals:** Allocate funds to achieve short-term goals, such as vacations, home renovations, or purchasing a vehicle. These goals may have specific timelines and can benefit from targeted savings.

- **Long-Term Goals:** Dedicate a portion of your income to long-term goals, such as retirement or your children's education. The earlier you start saving for these objectives, the more time your money has to grow.

- **Automate Savings:** To make saving a seamless process, automate transfers from your checking account to dedicated savings accounts for each goal. This ensures that savings occur consistently.

2. Gradual Investment: As your savings grow, consider transitioning a portion of these funds into investments. Investments offer the potential for higher returns, helping your money grow more rapidly than traditional savings accounts. Explore investment options that align with your risk tolerance and financial objectives.

Investing is a powerful strategy for growing your wealth over the long term. It involves putting your money to work in assets that have the potential to appreciate in value or generate income. Here's how you can gradually incorporate investment into your financial plan:

- **Assess Risk Tolerance:** Before investing, evaluate your risk tolerance. Consider factors like your investment horizon, financial goals, and comfort level with market fluctuations. Your risk tolerance will influence your investment choices.

- **Diversification:** Diversify your investments to spread risk and potentially enhance returns.

Diversification involves investing in a mix of asset classes like stocks, bonds, and real estate. Different asset classes behave differently under various market conditions, which can help mitigate losses during downturns.

- **Start Small:** If you're new to investing, consider beginning with a small amount of capital to gain experience and confidence. Many investment platforms offer fractional shares, allowing you to invest in high-priced assets with smaller amounts of money.

- **Educate Yourself:** Take the time to educate yourself about different investment options.

Chapter 5: Value Investing Demystified

Value investing stands as a beacon of financial wisdom in an often tumultuous world of investments. It has earned its place as a respected and time-tested approach to wealth creation, thanks in large part to the philosophies and successes of legendary investors like Benjamin Graham and Warren Buffett. In this chapter, we embark on a journey to demystify value investing, peeling back the layers to reveal its core principles and uncovering how it seamlessly integrates with the vital concept of asset allocation. By the end of this chapter, you'll possess a profound understanding of the art and science of value investing and its role in fortifying your family's financial stability.

Introduction to Value Investing

Value investing, in its essence, is akin to a treasure hunt within the vast landscape of financial markets. At its heart, it's the art of seeking out opportunities where assets are priced below their intrinsic value. This is not a game of chance but a deliberate and methodical approach that hinges on the belief that the market occasionally makes mistakes in pricing stocks and other assets. When these mispricings occur, they represent openings for savvy investors to seize.

To embark on this journey of value investing understanding, let's first dissect its core tenets:

1. Intrinsic Value: At the heart of value investing lies the concept of intrinsic value. This represents the true, underlying worth of an investment. Determining intrinsic value involves a deep dive into factors such as a company's financial health, earnings potential, competitive positioning, and long-term growth prospects. When the market price of an asset falls below its intrinsic value, it signals a potential opportunity for value investors.

2. Margin of Safety: Benjamin Graham, affectionately known as the "father of value investing," introduced the concept of a margin of safety. This concept is the bedrock of value investing, emphasizing the acquisition of assets at a substantial discount to their intrinsic value. The idea here is to build in a cushion, a safety net if you will, that guards against unforeseen market volatility or downturns. In essence, it's akin to buying a dollar for fifty cents.

3. Long-Term Perspective: Value investors are distinguished by their unwavering commitment to the long term. They possess the patience and discipline to hold their investments for extended periods. This protracted horizon allows time for the market to recognize and rectify mispricings, a hallmark of successful value investing.

4. Fundamental Analysis: Value investors are ardent practitioners of fundamental analysis. They diligently scrutinize a company's financial statements, competitive positioning within its industry, prevailing industry trends, and the quality of its management. This comprehensive assessment serves as the foundation for evaluating the intrinsic value of an investment.

5. Contrarian Approach: Value investors often adopt a contrarian mindset. In times of market exuberance and euphoria, when prices are inflated and optimism prevails, value investors may exercise caution and prudence. Conversely, during periods of market pessimism and despondency, when prices are depressed and negativity reigns, value investors see opportunity amid the despair.

Value Investing and Asset Allocation

Now that we've uncovered the essence of value investing, let's explore how it harmonizes with asset allocation—a pivotal aspect of building financial stability:

1. Diversification Through Value Investing:
Diversification is a cornerstone of sound investment strategy. Value investing can be a valuable component of a diversified investment portfolio. By incorporating value-oriented assets into your investment mix, you gain diversification benefits. Value stocks often exhibit distinct risk-return profiles compared to growth stocks, providing balance and risk mitigation within your overall portfolio.

Diversification is the practice of spreading your investments across various asset classes and investments to reduce risk. It's like not putting all your eggs in one basket. Value investing can contribute to diversification by providing exposure to assets with unique characteristics compared to other investment types.

2. Aligning with Financial Goals: A well-thought-out investment strategy considers your financial goals within the context of asset allocation. Value investing can be tailored to align with specific financial objectives within your asset allocation strategy. For instance, you might allocate a portion of your investments to value stocks with a long-term horizon, aiming for both capital appreciation and wealth preservation.

When determining your asset allocation, it's essential to align it with your financial goals. If one of your objectives is long-term wealth accumulation, value stocks, with their potential for growth and preservation of capital, can be a strategic choice.

3. Risk Management: The value investing philosophy inherently integrates risk management principles. By insisting on a margin of safety, value investors reduce the risk of capital loss. In essence, the margin of safety serves as a financial cushion that provides protection against unexpected market volatility or downturns.

Risk management is a critical aspect of investment strategy. Value investing incorporates a margin of safety, which can help safeguard your investments in times of market turbulence. This conservative approach can enhance risk management within your overall asset allocation.

4. Long-Term Wealth Building: One of the primary objectives of value investing is long-term wealth creation. This harmonizes seamlessly with the goal of building financial stability. When value-oriented assets appreciate over time, they contribute to the growth of your investment portfolio, laying the foundation for financial stability and future financial needs.

Building long-term wealth is often a central goal for families. Value investing's emphasis on a patient and disciplined approach aligns with this objective. Over the long haul, value-oriented investments can appreciate significantly, bolstering your family's financial stability.

5. Asset Allocation Rebalancing: Value investing can be an integral part of your asset allocation rebalancing strategy. If value stocks outperform other asset classes in your portfolio, periodic rebalancing can help maintain your desired asset allocation proportions. Rebalancing ensures that your portfolio stays aligned with your risk tolerance and long-term goals.

Asset allocation rebalancing is an essential practice to ensure that your investment portfolio maintains its intended risk profile over time. Value investing, as one of the components of your allocation, can benefit from periodic adjustments to optimize your overall portfolio.

It's important to note that value investing is just one of many investment approaches available. Your asset allocation should consider your overall investment goals, risk tolerance, and time horizon. It's advisable to consult with a financial advisor to develop an asset allocation strategy that incorporates value investing in a way that suits your unique financial circumstances.

In summary, value investing is an art and science that seeks opportunities where assets are undervalued. When seamlessly integrated into an asset allocation strategy, it can enhance diversification, risk management, and the potential for long-term wealth creation. As you continue your journey toward financial stability, consider how value investing aligns with your family's financial goals and preferences. Value investing is a timeless approach that has withstood the test of time, and it may hold the key to achieving your financial aspirations.

Part III: How to enable your children to become financially independent before they turn 45 years old

Chapter 6: Setting Up Investment Accounts

As you embark on the journey of enabling your children to achieve financial independence, it's imperative to lay the groundwork for their financial future. One of the foundational steps in this process is setting up investment accounts. In this chapter, we will explore the intricacies of establishing these accounts for your children, with a keen focus on asset allocation — the art of strategically dividing investments to optimize growth and mitigate risk.

Opening Investment Accounts for Your Children

Investment accounts for your children serve as the vehicles through which you can nurture their financial independence. These accounts offer a powerful means to accumulate wealth over time, providing them with a solid financial foundation as they progress towards adulthood. Here's how you can initiate this crucial step:

1. Research Account Types: Begin by researching the various types of investment accounts available for children. Common options include custodial accounts, 529 plans (for education savings), and even regular brokerage accounts held in trust. Each type has its unique features and tax implications, so it's essential to choose the one that aligns with your goals and financial circumstances.

2. Select a Suitable Provider: Once you've identified the type of investment account that suits your needs, research and choose a reputable financial institution or brokerage to host the account. Consider factors such as fees, account management options, and investment choices. Your choice of provider can significantly impact the growth of your child's wealth over time.

3. Complete the Account Setup: The process of opening an investment account typically involves providing personal information, including your child's Social Security number, and completing the necessary paperwork. Ensure that you adhere to all legal requirements and account ownership regulations.

4. Choose Appropriate Investments: With the account established, it's time to allocate assets. Depending on your child's age and your investment horizon, you can select a mix of investments that align with your goals. This might include stocks, bonds, mutual funds, or exchange-traded funds (ETFs). Your choice should reflect your risk tolerance and your child's time horizon.

5. Monitor and Manage: Setting up the account is just the beginning. Regularly monitor and manage the investments within the account. As your child grows, their investment strategy and goals may evolve, necessitating adjustments to the asset allocation. Stay informed about market conditions and make informed decisions to optimize the account's growth.

Asset Allocation in Investment Accounts

Asset allocation is the compass that guides your investment journey, helping you navigate the complex terrain of financial markets. It involves distributing your investments among different asset classes, such as stocks, bonds, and cash equivalents, with the aim of optimizing returns while managing risk. Here's how to approach asset allocation within your children's investment accounts:

1. Assess Risk Tolerance: Consider your child's risk tolerance when designing the asset allocation. Younger children with longer investment horizons may have a higher risk tolerance, allowing for a more aggressive allocation with a greater emphasis on stocks. As they approach adulthood, you might gradually shift towards a more balanced allocation to preserve wealth.

2. Diversify Wisely: Diversification is a fundamental principle of asset allocation. It involves spreading investments across different asset classes to reduce the impact of any single investment's poor performance on the overall portfolio. Diversification can help mitigate risk and enhance the potential for stable, long-term growth.

3. Time Horizon Matters: The time horizon, or the length of time until your child intends to access the funds, is a crucial factor in asset allocation. Longer time horizons allow for a more aggressive allocation, whereas shorter horizons may require a more conservative approach to protect capital.

4. Rebalance Periodically: Over time, the performance of different assets within your child's investment account may cause the allocation to drift from your desired target. Periodically review and rebalance the portfolio to realign it with your asset allocation goals. Rebalancing ensures that risk levels remain in check and that the portfolio continues to reflect your child's evolving financial goals.

5. Consider Tax Implications: Be mindful of the tax implications associated with asset allocation decisions. Different asset classes have varying tax treatments, and the tax efficiency of your child's investments can impact the overall return. Consult with a tax advisor or financial planner to optimize tax efficiency within the investment account.

6. Education and Involvement: As your child grows, involve them in discussions about their investment account. Educate them about asset allocation, risk, and the importance of a long-term perspective. This involvement can empower them to take an active role in managing their financial future.

Setting up investment accounts for your children and navigating the complexities of asset allocation is a critical step in enabling their journey towards financial independence. These accounts can serve as the wealth-building engines that support their aspirations and provide them with the financial stability to thrive in adulthood.

Remember that the path to financial independence is a gradual one, and investment accounts are a vital component of that journey. By carefully selecting the right account type, diligently managing investments, and thoughtfully designing asset allocation strategies, you can lay the foundation for your children's financial success. In the following chapters, we will delve deeper into investment strategies and financial principles that will further enrich the "Wealth Nest Egg Blueprint" and empower your children to achieve financial independence before turning 45 years old.

Chapter 7: Creating a Wealth Growth Strategy

In your quest to enable your children to achieve financial independence, a well-crafted wealth growth strategy is the linchpin that can turn aspirations into reality. This chapter delves into the intricacies of building a robust strategy for wealth accumulation. We'll explore the importance of developing a long-term investment strategy and draw insights from real-world case studies of successful asset allocators. By the end of this chapter, you'll be equipped with the knowledge and inspiration to forge your family's path to financial independence.

Developing a Long-Term Investment Strategy

A long-term investment strategy is the cornerstone of wealth creation. It provides a roadmap that guides your financial decisions and ensures that you stay the course even when faced with market fluctuations and economic cycles. Here's how to develop a resilient long-term investment strategy:

1. Clarify Your Financial Goals: Start by articulating your family's financial goals clearly. These goals may include milestones like funding your children's education, securing a comfortable retirement, or building generational wealth. Defining your objectives serves as the compass that directs your investment strategy.

2. Determine Your Investment Horizon: Your investment horizon is the length of time you plan to hold your investments before needing access to the funds. For children, this horizon can span decades, providing the luxury of time for compound growth. A longer investment horizon typically allows for a more aggressive asset allocation, which can yield higher returns over time.

3. Assess Risk Tolerance: Understanding your risk tolerance is crucial in shaping your investment strategy. Risk tolerance is a measure of your willingness and capacity to endure market volatility. It's essential to align your asset allocation with your risk tolerance to ensure that you can stay committed to your strategy during periods of market turbulence.

4. Design Your Asset Allocation: Asset allocation is the process of dividing your investments among different asset classes, such as stocks, bonds, real estate, and cash equivalents. The allocation should reflect your financial goals, risk tolerance, and investment horizon. Younger children's accounts may favor a higher allocation to stocks for long-term growth, while approaching adulthood may prompt a more balanced allocation.

5. Diversify Effectively: Diversification is a key risk management tool in your investment arsenal. It involves spreading your investments across various assets to reduce the impact of poor performance in any single investment. Effective diversification can help mitigate risk while optimizing potential returns. Consider diversifying across asset classes, industries, and geographic regions.

6. Stay the Course: A long-term investment strategy requires discipline and a commitment to staying the course. It's important to resist the urge to make impulsive decisions based on short-term market fluctuations. Regularly review your portfolio to ensure alignment with your strategy, but avoid knee-jerk reactions to market noise.

7. Periodic Rebalancing: Over time, the performance of different assets within your portfolio may cause your asset allocation to deviate from your target. Periodic rebalancing is the process of realigning your portfolio with your desired asset allocation. This practice helps manage risk and maintain the intended balance of your investments.

Case Studies of Successful Asset Allocators

Learning from the experiences of successful asset allocators can provide valuable insights into crafting your family's wealth growth strategy. Let's delve into a few case studies that illustrate the principles of effective asset allocation:

Case Study 1: Warren Buffett

Warren Buffett, often regarded as one of the greatest investors of all time, has built his wealth through a disciplined and patient approach to asset allocation. His strategy is rooted in value investing, which involves identifying undervalued companies and holding them for the long term. Buffett's success underscores the importance of staying committed to a well-defined investment philosophy and taking a long-term perspective.

Case Study 2: Endowment Funds

Many university endowment funds have achieved remarkable long-term investment success through diversified asset allocation. These institutions allocate their assets across a wide range of investments, including equities, fixed income, alternative investments, and real estate. Their approach illustrates the benefits of diversification and the advantages of a long investment horizon.

Case Study 3: Family Dynasties

Several wealthy family dynasties have sustained and grown their wealth over multiple generations. Their success often stems from a structured approach to wealth preservation and growth. These families typically employ a mix of asset classes, including stocks, bonds, real estate, and private investments, to achieve their financial goals. Their stories emphasize the significance of intergenerational planning and asset allocation.

These case studies highlight the diverse ways in which successful asset allocators have approached wealth growth. While their specific strategies may vary, common threads include a clear investment philosophy, diversification, and a long-term perspective. By drawing inspiration from these examples and tailoring them to your family's unique circumstances and goals, you can create a wealth growth strategy that aligns with your vision of financial independence for your children.

As you embark on the journey of crafting your family's wealth growth strategy, remember that it's not a one-size-fits-all endeavor. Your strategy should be dynamic, adaptable, and rooted in your family's financial aspirations. With a clear sense of your goals, a well-defined investment philosophy, and a commitment to a long-term perspective, you can chart a course toward financial independence that paves the way for your children to thrive. In the chapters that follow, we will delve deeper into specific investment strategies and tactics that will further enrich your family's "Wealth Nest Egg Blueprint."

Part IV: Nurturing Financial Discipline

Chapter 8: Teaching Financial Discipline

Financial discipline is the bedrock upon which financial independence is built. In this chapter, we delve into the art of instilling good financial habits in your children and maintaining discipline when allocating funds to assets. These skills will empower your children to navigate the complex world of finance with confidence and competence, setting them on a path to lasting financial success.

Strategies for Instilling Good Financial Habits

Teaching your children good financial habits is one of the most valuable gifts you can bestow upon them. Here are strategies to cultivate financial discipline from an early age:

1. Financial Education: Begin with the basics of financial education. Equip your children with the knowledge they need to understand money, budgeting, saving, investing, and the power of compounding. Encourage them to ask questions and explore financial concepts. Consider introducing age-appropriate books and resources that make learning about money engaging and accessible.

2. Lead by Example: Children learn by observing. Demonstrate responsible financial behavior in your own life. Be transparent about financial decisions and share the reasoning behind them. Your actions serve as a powerful model for financial discipline. When your children witness prudent financial choices in action, they are more likely to emulate them.

3. Allowance and Budgeting: Consider providing your children with an allowance, tying it to age-appropriate responsibilities. Encourage them to budget their allowance, allocating funds for spending, saving, and giving. This practice helps them understand the importance of managing money wisely and prioritizing their financial goals. Allow them to make spending decisions within their budget to develop financial responsibility.

4. Goal Setting: Teach your children to set financial goals. Whether it's saving for a coveted toy, funding a college education, or investing for the future, setting goals instills a sense of purpose and discipline in managing money. Help them break down larger financial objectives into achievable milestones, emphasizing the rewards of diligent saving and investing.

5. Delayed Gratification: Emphasize the value of delayed gratification. Encourage your children to save for larger purchases rather than succumbing to instant gratification. This habit fosters patience and discipline, helping them appreciate the satisfaction of achieving long-term goals through disciplined saving and investing.

6. Money Management Tools: Introduce your children to basic money management tools, such as piggy banks, savings accounts, and budgeting apps designed for kids. These tools can make financial concepts tangible and accessible, allowing your children to track their progress and learn valuable money management skills.

7. Entrepreneurial Skills: Encourage entrepreneurial endeavors. Whether it's a lemonade stand, selling handmade crafts, or mowing lawns, entrepreneurial experiences teach the principles of earning, saving, and managing money. These early ventures instill a sense of financial empowerment and resourcefulness.

8. Financial Literacy Resources: Utilize age-appropriate financial literacy resources. Books, games, and online courses designed for children can make learning about money engaging and fun. Explore interactive tools and games that teach financial concepts while entertaining your children.

9. Open Dialogue: Maintain open and ongoing conversations about money. Create a safe space for your children to ask questions, seek guidance, and share their financial concerns. Encourage them to express their financial aspirations and dreams, fostering a sense of ownership and responsibility for their financial future.

Discipline in Allocating Funds to Assets

Financial discipline extends beyond the realm of personal finance; it encompasses the allocation of funds to assets that appreciate over time. Instilling discipline in this aspect is essential for achieving financial independence.

1. Asset Allocation Strategy: Review and revisit your asset allocation strategy regularly. Ensure that it aligns with your family's financial goals, risk tolerance, and investment horizon. Make adjustments as needed to stay on course. A well-considered asset allocation strategy serves as the compass that guides your family's wealth-building journey.

2. Automation: Automate your investments whenever possible. Set up automatic contributions to investment accounts, retirement funds, and other assets. Automation reduces the temptation to divert funds away from savings and investments, ensuring that your financial goals remain a priority. It eliminates the need for active decision-making and reinforces a disciplined savings habit.

3. Emergency Fund: Maintain a well-funded emergency fund. This financial cushion provides peace of mind and prevents the need to dip into long-term investments during unexpected financial setbacks. The discipline of preserving an emergency fund safeguards your family's financial stability and ensures that your investment strategy remains intact.

4. Resist Impulse Spending: Encourage disciplined spending habits within your family. Distinguish between needs and wants, and emphasize the importance of responsible consumption. Avoid impulse purchases that can divert funds from savings and investments. Teach your children to think critically before making spending decisions, reinforcing the principle of prioritizing long-term financial goals.

5. Periodic Review: Conduct periodic reviews of your financial goals and progress. Assess whether you are adhering to your asset allocation and savings plan. Reflect on any adjustments needed to maintain discipline and stay aligned with your family's financial objectives. Regularly reviewing your financial plan keeps your goals in focus and helps you adapt to changing circumstances.

6. Reinforce the Long-Term Perspective: Remind your children, and yourself, of the long-term perspective. Investing for financial independence is a marathon, not a sprint. Maintain discipline even in the face of short-term market fluctuations or economic uncertainties. Emphasize the importance of staying committed to your investment strategy over time to reap the rewards of compounding and asset appreciation.

7. Professional Guidance: Consider seeking professional guidance from financial advisors. They can provide expert insights, help tailor your investment strategy to your family's unique circumstances, and keep you accountable to your financial goals. A financial advisor can assist in optimizing your asset allocation and maintaining discipline in your wealth-building journey.

8. Family Commitment: Engage your family in discussions about financial discipline and the shared commitment to your financial goals. Ensure that everyone in the family is aligned with your financial plan and understands the importance of adhering to a disciplined approach. When the entire family is committed to financial discipline, it becomes a collective effort that reinforces your financial stability and success.

By imparting the principles of financial discipline and demonstrating their application in both personal finance and asset allocation, you equip your children with essential life skills. These skills will serve them well on their journey to financial independence, ensuring that they make informed decisions, remain committed to their financial goals, and navigate the complexities of the financial world with resilience and confidence.

In the following chapters, we will continue to explore advanced investment strategies, wealth preservation techniques, and the importance of adapting to changing financial landscapes. Through continued learning and disciplined financial practices, your family's path to financial independence will become a reality.

Part V: Passing on the Knowledge

Chapter 9: Passing on the Knowledge

The journey towards financial independence is not just about achieving personal financial success — it's about equipping the next generation with the knowledge and skills they need to thrive. In this final part of "How to enable your children to become financially independent before they turn 45 years old," we explore the critical importance of passing on financial knowledge to your children. We'll delve into the significance of financial education and provide guidance on age-appropriate financial lessons. By imparting these valuable insights, you empower your children to build upon the foundation you've laid and continue the legacy of financial independence.

The Importance of Financial Education

Financial education is a lifelong gift that keeps on giving. It equips individuals with the tools they need to make informed financial decisions, manage money wisely, and secure their financial future. Here's why financial education is a cornerstone of your family's path to financial independence:

1. Empowerment: Financial education empowers individuals to take control of their financial lives. It provides them with the knowledge and confidence to make sound financial decisions that align with their goals and values. The sense of empowerment that comes with financial literacy is invaluable, enabling individuals to navigate life's financial challenges with resilience and determination.

2. Decision-Making Skills: Financial education enhances decision-making skills. It equips individuals with the ability to assess financial options, evaluate risks, and choose strategies that maximize their financial well-being. In a world filled with complex financial choices, the ability to make informed decisions is a skill that serves individuals throughout their lives.

3. Financial Security: A strong foundation in financial education contributes to financial security. It helps individuals plan for emergencies, save for goals, and build a safety net that safeguards their financial stability. Financial security provides peace of mind, ensuring that individuals can weather unexpected financial storms without jeopardizing their long-term financial plans.

4. Long-Term Wealth Building: Financial education fosters a mindset of long-term wealth building. It instills the principles of saving, investing, and asset allocation, enabling individuals to grow their wealth over time. This long-term perspective is crucial for achieving financial independence and generational wealth.

5. Legacy Building: Passing on financial knowledge to the next generation is a powerful way to build a lasting legacy of financial success. It ensures that your family's wealth-building journey continues for generations to come. By instilling financial education in your children, you contribute to the sustainability of your family's financial well-being and create opportunities for future prosperity.

Age-Appropriate Financial Lessons

Financial education should be tailored to an individual's age and developmental stage. Here are age-appropriate financial lessons to consider as you guide your children towards financial independence:

Early Childhood (Ages 3-6):

- **Basic Money Concepts:** Introduce simple concepts like the value of coins and bills. Teach them how to identify different denominations. Use playful activities and games to make learning enjoyable.

- **Saving:** Encourage saving by using piggy banks or jars. Explain the concept of setting aside money for future use. Help them understand the idea that saving today can lead to more significant opportunities in the future.

Elementary School (Ages 7-12):

- **Budgeting:** Teach them the basics of budgeting by allocating allowance or money from chores to different categories like spending, saving, and giving. Create a visual budget with them, such as a spreadsheet or simple budgeting app.

- **Needs vs. Wants:** Discuss the difference between needs (essential expenses) and wants (non-essential items). Help them prioritize needs over wants and make conscious spending choices.

- **Entrepreneurship:** Encourage entrepreneurial ventures like a lemonade stand or selling crafts to instill the principles of earning and managing money. Guide them through the process, from setting prices to tracking expenses and profits.

Teenagers (Ages 13-18):

- **Banking:** Introduce the concepts of checking and savings accounts. Teach them how to manage a bank account and track transactions. Help them understand the importance of monitoring account balances and avoiding overdrafts.

- **Credit and Debt:** Explain the basics of credit, interest rates, and the consequences of debt. Discuss responsible credit card use, emphasizing the importance of paying bills on time and in full to avoid high-interest charges.

- **Investing:** Introduce the concept of investing and the power of compounding. Consider opening a custodial investment account for them to manage. Explain various investment options, such as stocks, bonds, and mutual funds.

Young Adults (Ages 18 and Older):

- **Financial Independence:** Discuss the transition to financial independence, including budgeting, paying bills, and managing expenses. Encourage them to create their budget and handle their financial responsibilities.

- **Taxes:** Explain how taxes work, including income tax and deductions. Teach them how to file a tax return and the importance of fulfilling tax obligations accurately and on time.

- **Estate Planning:** Discuss the importance of wills, trusts, and estate planning for the preservation and transfer of wealth. Encourage them to consider their long-term financial goals and how estate planning fits into their overall financial strategy.

Continual Learning (All Ages):

- **Investment Strategies:** Explore advanced investment strategies, asset allocation, and portfolio management as they mature and take on more financial responsibilities. Discuss the benefits of diversification and the importance of staying informed about market developments.

- **Financial Literacy Resources:** Encourage them to continue learning through books, courses, and resources that deepen their financial knowledge. Point them towards reputable sources of financial information and encourage critical thinking when evaluating financial advice.

Passing on financial knowledge is an ongoing process that adapts to your children's evolving needs and circumstances. By providing age-appropriate financial lessons and fostering a culture of financial education within your family, you ensure that your children are well-equipped to navigate the complexities of the financial world and continue the legacy of financial independence that you've built.

In the final chapters of this book, we will explore advanced financial strategies, legacy planning, and the significance of generational wealth. As you pass on your knowledge and empower your children, you set the stage for a prosperous and secure financial future that extends far beyond your own lifetime.

Chapter 10: Monitoring and Adjusting

Financial independence is not a static destination; it's an ongoing journey that requires vigilance, adaptability, and active management of your financial resources. In this chapter, we delve into the critical aspects of monitoring and adjusting your financial plan. We'll explore how to track and manage your investment portfolio effectively and discuss the role of asset allocation in portfolio management. By mastering these skills, you'll ensure that your family's wealth continues to grow, and your path to financial independence remains on course.

Tracking and Managing the Investment Portfolio

Effective portfolio management begins with a clear understanding of your investment goals and a commitment to monitoring and managing your investments proactively. Here's how to navigate this essential aspect of your financial journey:

1. Set Clear Objectives: Revisit your financial goals and investment objectives regularly. Ensure that your portfolio aligns with your goals, risk tolerance, and investment horizon. Whether your aim is wealth accumulation, retirement planning, or generational wealth transfer, your investment strategy should reflect these goals. Clear objectives serve as the guiding stars that steer your investment decisions.

2. Regularly Review Holdings: Conduct periodic reviews of your investment holdings. Examine the performance of individual assets within your portfolio. Are they meeting your expectations, or are adjustments needed? Be prepared to make changes if an asset no longer aligns with your financial plan. A thoughtful review process helps you identify opportunities and challenges within your portfolio.

3. Monitor Asset Allocation: Asset allocation is a cornerstone of successful portfolio management. Regularly assess your asset allocation to ensure it remains in line with your desired risk-return profile. Rebalance your portfolio if necessary to maintain your target allocation. Asset allocation acts as the compass that keeps your portfolio heading in the right direction.

4. Risk Management: Continuously evaluate the risk within your portfolio. Understand the risk characteristics of each asset class and investment. Consider how changes in the economic and market landscape may impact your investments. Adjust your portfolio to mitigate undue risk exposure. Effective risk management safeguards your financial stability.

5. Cost Control: Be mindful of investment costs. High fees and expenses can erode your returns over time. Review the fees associated with your investments, and consider low-cost index funds or exchange-traded funds (ETFs) as cost-efficient alternatives. Cost-conscious investing ensures that a greater share of your returns stays in your pocket.

6. Tax Efficiency: Keep tax efficiency in mind when managing your portfolio. Explore tax-advantaged accounts and strategies to minimize your tax liabilities. Consider the tax implications of buying, selling, or holding investments. Tax-aware investing optimizes your after-tax returns.

7. Stay Informed: Stay informed about economic and market developments that may affect your investments. Read financial news, follow market trends, and consider seeking advice from financial professionals when needed. Informed decision-making positions you to react thoughtfully to changing market conditions.

8. Record Keeping: Maintain organized records of your investments, transactions, and performance. This documentation helps track progress and simplifies tax reporting. Digital tools and portfolio management software can streamline this process, saving you time and effort.

Asset Allocation in Portfolio Management

Asset allocation is the strategic distribution of your investments among different asset classes, such as stocks, bonds, real estate, and cash equivalents. It plays a pivotal role in portfolio management and significantly influences your investment outcomes. Here's how to navigate the intricacies of asset allocation:

1. Diversification: Diversify your investments across multiple asset classes. Diversification reduces the impact of poor performance in any single investment and spreads risk. Consider the historical performance and correlation between asset classes when building a diversified portfolio. Diversification is your shield against concentration risk.

2. Risk-Return Trade-Off: Understand the risk-return trade-off inherent in asset allocation. Generally, assets with higher potential returns also carry higher levels of risk. Balance your asset allocation to align with your risk tolerance and investment horizon. The trade-off is the fulcrum on which your portfolio's risk and return pivot.

3. Time Horizon: Consider your investment time horizon when determining asset allocation. Longer time horizons may allow for a more aggressive allocation to growth assets, such as stocks, while shorter horizons may require a more conservative allocation to preserve capital. Time horizon tailors your allocation to your financial journey's timeline.

4. Regular Rebalancing: Periodically review your portfolio's asset allocation and rebalance it if necessary. Rebalancing involves selling assets that have outperformed and buying assets that have underperformed to restore your target allocation. This practice maintains your desired risk level and aligns with your investment goals. Rebalancing is your compass realignment.

5. Age and Life Stage: Your age and life stage should influence your asset allocation. Younger investors with a longer time horizon may allocate a larger portion of their portfolio to stocks for growth. As you approach retirement or other financial milestones, consider adjusting your allocation to reduce risk. Age and life stage customize your allocation to your evolving needs.

6. Seek Professional Advice: If you are uncertain about asset allocation or portfolio management, consider seeking advice from a financial advisor. An advisor can help you tailor your allocation to your specific goals, risk tolerance, and financial circumstances. Professional guidance provides valuable insights into optimizing your allocation.

Effective monitoring and adjusting of your investment portfolio are vital for preserving and growing your wealth. By staying vigilant, making informed decisions, and proactively managing your assets, you position yourself to achieve and maintain financial independence. Monitoring and adjusting are your compass and navigation tools that keep you on the right financial course.

In the concluding chapters of this book, we will explore advanced investment strategies, legacy planning, and the significance of generational wealth. As you continue on your journey towards financial independence, remember that it's not just about reaching the destination—it's about maintaining and expanding the legacy of financial success you've built for your family.

Part VI: Overcoming Challenges

Chapter 11: Success Stories

As we near the conclusion of "How to enable your children to become financially independent before they turn 45 years old," it's essential to draw inspiration from those who have successfully achieved early financial independence. In this chapter, we'll explore inspiring stories of individuals and families who have managed to break free from the traditional financial constraints and attain financial freedom at a young age. We'll also delve into the pivotal role that asset allocation played in their remarkable success stories. By learning from these examples, you can gain valuable insights and strategies to overcome your own financial challenges on the path to independence.

Inspiring Stories of Early Financial Independence

Early financial independence, often referred to as "FIRE" (Financial Independence, Retire Early), has become a movement that showcases individuals who have achieved financial freedom well before the traditional retirement age. These success stories demonstrate that with dedication, discipline, and strategic planning, it is possible to break free from the paycheck-to-paycheck cycle and live life on your terms.

1. The Minimalist Maven: Sarah's Journey

Sarah, a true minimalist, embraced a frugal lifestyle as a deliberate choice to expedite her path to financial independence. She understood that reducing her expenses would free up more resources for strategic asset allocation. By living well below her means and investing wisely in a diversified portfolio of low-cost index funds, she achieved financial independence at the age of 35.

Sarah's story is a testament to the power of simplicity and disciplined saving. Her minimalist lifestyle not only minimized her financial burdens but also reinforced the importance of asset allocation in building wealth. By keeping her expenses low, she had more capital to allocate to her investments, accelerating her journey to financial freedom.

2. The Entrepreneur Extraordinaire: John's Triumph

John, a serial entrepreneur, embarked on a journey that led him to multiple business successes. His passion for technology translated into a series of profitable startups. However, what set John apart was not just his entrepreneurial spirit but also his astute asset allocation strategies.

Recognizing that business ventures can be unpredictable, John allocated a portion of his income to various investment vehicles. This diversified approach ensured that he didn't rely solely on his entrepreneurial endeavors for wealth accumulation. Instead, he continuously reinvested profits while simultaneously managing his investment portfolio. This dual strategy allowed him to reach financial independence in his early 40s.

John's story highlights the importance of having multiple income streams and how strategic asset allocation can complement entrepreneurial endeavors. His journey shows that diversifying investments can provide stability and consistent growth, even in the volatile world of startups.

3. The Real Estate Visionary: Emily and Michael's Achievement

Emily and Michael, a married couple, chose real estate as their primary wealth-building strategy. Over the years, they strategically acquired rental properties, diligently managed their portfolio, and used rental income and property appreciation to achieve financial freedom in their late 40s.

Their journey showcases the value of diversification and asset allocation within a specific asset class. While they focused on real estate, they didn't put all their eggs in one basket. Instead, they diversified within the real estate market by acquiring different types of properties in various locations. This approach helped mitigate risks associated with a single investment.

Emily and Michael's story underscores how asset allocation is not limited to traditional investments like stocks and bonds. Within each asset class, there are opportunities for diversification and strategic allocation. By adapting their asset allocation strategy as they expanded their real estate portfolio, they achieved their financial goals and secured their independence.

The Role of Asset Allocation in Their Success

While these success stories vary in approach, they all share a common thread—the strategic allocation of assets played a pivotal role in achieving financial independence. Here's how asset allocation contributed to their success:

Risk Mitigation: Asset allocation helped spread risk across different investments. This diversification reduced the impact of poor-performing assets and market volatility, preserving and growing their wealth over time.

Consistent Growth: A well-structured asset allocation strategy provided consistent growth potential. By strategically balancing riskier assets (e.g., stocks) with more stable assets (e.g., bonds or real estate), they maintained steady portfolio growth.

Adaptability: Asset allocation allowed them to adapt to changing financial circumstances and goals. As their financial situation evolved, they adjusted their allocation to align with new objectives, whether that was wealth preservation or income generation.

Long-Term Focus: Successful individuals recognized that asset allocation is a long-term strategy. They resisted the temptation to make impulsive changes based on short-term market fluctuations and instead remained committed to their allocation strategy.

Income Generation: In some cases, asset allocation favored income generation through investments like dividend-paying stocks or rental properties. This income provided financial security and reduced the need for traditional employment.

By studying these success stories and understanding the role of asset allocation in their achievements, you gain valuable insights into the possibilities of early financial independence. While their paths may differ, the principles of disciplined saving, strategic investing, and smart asset allocation are universal.

In the final chapters of this book, we will explore advanced financial strategies, legacy planning, and the significance of generational wealth. Armed with the knowledge of these inspiring success stories, you'll be better equipped to overcome challenges and chart your own course toward financial independence. Remember that every financial journey is unique, and with the right strategies and determination, you can turn your financial goals into reality.

Chapter 12: Overcoming Challenges

As you embark on your journey towards financial independence and implement the wealth-building strategies outlined in this book, it's essential to recognize that challenges and setbacks are a natural part of the process. In this chapter, we will address common setbacks that individuals may encounter along the way and discuss the importance of staying committed to asset allocation as a foundational element of your financial plan. By understanding how to navigate obstacles and maintain your asset allocation strategy, you'll be better prepared to overcome challenges and continue progressing toward your financial goals.

Addressing Common Setbacks

Achieving financial independence is a significant undertaking, and it's not uncommon to encounter obstacles along the way. Let's delve deeper into these common setbacks and explore strategies for effectively addressing them:

1. Market Volatility: Navigating the Storms

Financial markets are inherently volatile, and investment values can fluctuate. During periods of market turbulence, it's crucial to avoid making emotional, knee-jerk reactions. Stick to your long-term asset allocation plan and resist the temptation to make drastic changes based on short-term market movements. Remember that market downturns can present buying opportunities for long-term investors.

Market volatility is a constant in the world of investing. It's important to have a well-thought-out plan in place to manage it. Your asset allocation strategy, tailored to your risk tolerance and investment horizon, acts as your anchor during turbulent times. By staying the course and focusing on the long-term, you can weather the storm of market volatility.

2. Unexpected Expenses: Preparing for the Unexpected

Life is full of unexpected expenses, such as medical emergencies, home repairs, or car breakdowns. While these events can disrupt your financial plans, having an emergency fund in place can provide a safety net. Ensure that your asset allocation includes a portion allocated to cash or cash equivalents to cover unforeseen expenses without derailing your long-term investments.

The unexpected is part of life, and financial planning should account for it. Your emergency fund, a critical component of your asset allocation, acts as a financial cushion. It ensures that you have readily accessible funds to address emergencies without resorting to liquidating long-term investments at inopportune times.

3. Changing Financial Goals: Evolving with Purpose

Over time, your financial goals may evolve. You may decide to start a business, pursue further education, or change your retirement timeline. It's essential to periodically reassess your goals and adjust your asset allocation strategy accordingly. Flexibility in asset allocation allows you to adapt to changing circumstances while staying on course.

Life is dynamic, and so are your financial goals. As you navigate various life stages and opportunities, your asset allocation should evolve with you. This adaptability ensures that your investments continue to align with your objectives, whether they involve growth, income, or capital preservation.

4. Emotional Biases: Mastering Emotional Intelligence

Emotional biases, such as fear or overconfidence, can lead to poor financial decisions. Recognize these biases and develop a disciplined approach to investment and asset allocation. Consider seeking advice from a financial advisor to help you remain objective and make rational decisions.

Emotions can be both allies and adversaries in financial decision-making. Recognizing and managing emotional biases is a crucial skill for investors. By adhering to a well-defined asset allocation plan and seeking objective advice when needed, you can harness emotional intelligence to make more informed choices.

5. Inflation: Protecting Your Purchasing Power

Inflation erodes the purchasing power of money over time. To combat inflation, it's important to include assets in your allocation that have the potential for growth and income generation. Stocks and real estate, for example, historically outpace inflation, helping your portfolio maintain its value over the long term.

Inflation is a silent wealth eroder, but you can defend against it with a well-crafted asset allocation. By incorporating assets that historically outpace inflation into your strategy, you preserve your purchasing power. This means your money retains its value and continues to work for you.

6. Behavioral Challenges: Mastering Discipline

Staying disciplined and sticking to your asset allocation plan can be challenging, especially during market downturns or periods of economic uncertainty. Develop a written investment policy statement that outlines your financial goals, risk tolerance, and asset allocation strategy. This document can serve as a reminder of your long-term plan and help you resist impulsive decisions.

Maintaining discipline is a cornerstone of successful investing. Your investment policy statement, a tangible representation of your asset allocation plan, serves as your compass. It keeps you on course, reminding you of your financial goals and the strategies you've established to achieve them.

Staying Committed to Asset Allocation

Amidst these challenges, your commitment to asset allocation remains a cornerstone of your financial success. Let's explore further why staying committed to asset allocation is crucial:

1. Risk Management: The Pillar of Diversification

Asset allocation helps manage risk by diversifying your investments across various asset classes. This diversification reduces the impact of underperforming assets, providing a degree of stability in your portfolio. Diversification is your risk management strategy, ensuring that the fortunes of one asset do not dictate your financial destiny.

2. Long-Term Growth: The Steady Ascent

A well-structured asset allocation strategy is designed for long-term growth. Even in the face of short-term setbacks, maintaining your allocation plan allows you to benefit from the growth potential of your investments over time. It's a marathon, not a sprint, and asset allocation is your training regimen for wealth accumulation.

3. Adaptability: The Shape-Shifting Ally

Asset allocation offers adaptability. As your financial circumstances change or new goals arise, you can adjust your allocation to align with your evolving needs. This flexibility ensures that your financial plan remains relevant and responsive to the dynamic nature of life.

4. Emotional Resilience: The Shield Against Impulsiveness

Sticking to a predetermined asset allocation plan can help you maintain emotional resilience during challenging times. By following a disciplined strategy, you're less likely to succumb to emotional biases that can lead to poor decisions. Your allocation plan provides a structured framework that shields you from impulsiveness.

5. Consistency: The Path to Success

Consistency in asset allocation ensures that you remain on track toward your financial goals. Regardless of external market forces or personal challenges, a steadfast commitment to your allocation plan provides a sense of stability. It's your financial roadmap, guiding you through the twists and turns of your journey.

6. Wealth Preservation: Safeguarding Your Legacy

Asset allocation plays a vital role in preserving your wealth. By carefully choosing a mix of assets that align with your objectives, you can minimize unnecessary risks and work toward protecting your financial well-being. It's your strategy for safeguarding the wealth you've accumulated.

As you encounter challenges on your journey to financial independence, remember that setbacks are opportunities for growth and learning. By addressing common setbacks and staying committed to your asset allocation strategy, you'll not only overcome obstacles but also strengthen your financial foundation. In the following chapters, we will explore advanced financial strategies, legacy planning, and the significance of generational wealth. Your commitment to asset allocation will continue to be a guiding principle as you build and safeguard your wealth for the future.

Part VII: Preparing for the Future

Chapter 13: Preparing for the Future

As we approach the conclusion of "How to enable your children to become financially independent before they turn 45 years old," it's essential to shift our focus towards preparing for the future — specifically, how to equip your children for financial responsibility and navigate responsible asset management and inheritance planning. In this chapter, we will explore strategies for instilling financial responsibility in the next generation and ensuring that your wealth is managed and passed on in a way that aligns with your values and goals. By preparing for the future, you lay the groundwork for the continued growth and preservation of your family's wealth.

Strategies for Preparing Children for Financial Responsibility

One of the most significant gifts you can give your children is a solid foundation in financial literacy and responsibility. Here are strategies to help prepare them for the financial challenges and opportunities they will face:

1. Early Education: Start teaching financial concepts from an early age. Use age-appropriate language and examples to introduce topics like saving, budgeting, and the importance of delayed gratification. Encourage questions and curiosity about money.

Financial education is a lifelong journey, and it begins in childhood. By introducing basic financial concepts early on, you provide your children with the building blocks for a lifetime of financial responsibility. Consider creating fun, interactive lessons that make learning about money engaging and relatable for kids.

2. Allowance and Budgeting: Consider providing your children with an allowance tied to responsibilities or tasks. This helps them learn the value of earned money and the importance of budgeting. Encourage them to allocate their funds for spending, saving, and giving.

An allowance can be a valuable tool for teaching financial responsibility. When children earn money through chores or tasks, they gain a sense of the effort required to earn income. Encourage them to create a budget that reflects their priorities, such as saving for a desired item, donating to a cause they care about, and covering their daily expenses.

3. Savings and Goals: Help your children set savings goals. Whether they're saving for a toy, a special outing, or their future education, having a goal reinforces the habit of saving. Open a savings account for them and involve them in the process.

Goal setting is a fundamental skill that extends into adulthood. Teach your children to define clear financial objectives and create a plan to achieve them. When they experience the satisfaction of reaching their savings goals, they'll be motivated to apply the same principles to more substantial financial milestones in the future.

4. Financial Discussions: Engage in age-appropriate financial discussions with your children. As they grow, involve them in family financial decisions, such as planning vacations, making purchases, or charitable giving. Share stories of your own financial successes and challenges to provide real-world context.

Open dialogue about money within the family fosters a healthy understanding of financial matters. Encourage your children to ask questions and express their thoughts and concerns about money. By involving them in financial decisions, you provide valuable insights into the decision-making process and demonstrate responsible financial stewardship.

5. Invest in Financial Education: Consider providing your children with access to financial education resources. There are many books, websites, and educational programs designed to teach children about money. Investing in their financial education can yield lifelong benefits.

Financial literacy resources tailored to children and teenagers are readily available. Explore books, online games, and workshops designed to make financial education engaging and relatable. Encourage your children to explore these resources independently and discuss what they've learned.

6. Lead by Example: Your behavior with money serves as a powerful example for your children. Demonstrate responsible financial habits, such as saving, budgeting, and charitable giving. Be open about your financial values and priorities.

Children learn by observing, and your financial behavior sets a powerful precedent. Strive to model the financial values and behaviors you wish to instill in your children. Whether it's saving a portion of your income, making thoughtful spending choices, or prioritizing charitable giving, your actions speak volumes about your financial philosophy.

Responsible Asset Management and Inheritance

Ensuring that your wealth is managed and passed on responsibly requires thoughtful planning and communication. Here are key considerations for responsible asset management and inheritance planning:

1. Define Your Values: Clearly define your values and principles regarding wealth management and inheritance. Consider what you want to achieve with your wealth, such as providing for your children's education, supporting charitable causes, or preserving family assets.

Values serve as the guiding principles for wealth management and inheritance planning. Take the time to reflect on your core values and how they align with your financial goals. This introspection will help you make decisions that resonate with your beliefs and priorities.

2. Estate Planning: Consult with legal and financial professionals to create a comprehensive estate plan. This plan should include a will, trusts, and other legal documents that specify how your assets should be distributed and managed after your passing.

Estate planning is a crucial aspect of responsible wealth management. Work closely with professionals who specialize in estate law and financial planning to ensure that your wishes are clearly documented and legally enforceable. Regularly review and update your estate plan to reflect changing circumstances.

3. Communication: Open and transparent communication with your heirs is crucial. Discuss your financial values, goals, and the responsibilities that come with inherited wealth. Encourage dialogue about their own financial aspirations and how your wealth can support their journey.

Fostering open communication within your family is vital for ensuring that your wealth is managed in accordance with your intentions. Schedule family meetings or discussions to address financial matters and provide a platform for questions and concerns. Encourage your heirs to express their views and share their financial goals.

4. Financial Education: Just as you received financial education, consider providing your heirs with the knowledge and tools they need to manage their inheritance wisely. Offer resources and guidance to help them navigate financial decisions.

Financial education is an ongoing process that extends beyond childhood. Support your heirs in their pursuit of financial knowledge and skills. Consider offering access to financial planning professionals who can provide personalized guidance and advice.

5. Stewardship: Encourage a sense of stewardship among your heirs. Teach them the importance of preserving and growing family wealth for future generations. Instill a sense of responsibility for managing assets in a way that aligns with your values.

Stewardship is the mindset that your wealth is not just for the present but also for future generations. Encourage your heirs to view themselves as custodians of your family's financial legacy. Emphasize the importance of responsible asset management and the duty to pass on the benefits of wealth to succeeding generations.

6. Professional Guidance: Consider involving financial advisors or trustees to assist with asset management and distribution. Professional guidance can ensure that your wealth is managed prudently and in accordance with your wishes.

Financial advisors and trustees play a vital role in implementing your wealth management and inheritance plan. Collaborate with professionals who have a thorough understanding of your financial goals and values. Regularly review the performance of these advisors to ensure they align with your objectives.

7. Philanthropic Legacy: If charitable giving is important to you, explore opportunities to establish a family foundation or charitable trust. Involving your heirs in philanthropic activities can instill a sense of purpose and responsibility.

Philanthropy is a meaningful way to pass on your values and create a lasting legacy. Consider involving your heirs in charitable initiatives, allowing them to participate in philanthropic decisions and activities. This experience can instill a sense of social responsibility and connect them to the broader community.

By implementing these strategies, you can help prepare your children for financial responsibility and ensure that your wealth is managed and passed on in a way that reflects your values and goals. In the following chapters, we will explore advanced financial strategies, legacy planning, and the significance of generational wealth. Your commitment to preparing for the future will contribute to the enduring prosperity and financial well-being of your family for generations to come.

Conclusion: Setting Your Children on a Path to Financial Independence

As we reach the conclusion of "How to enable your children to become financially independent before they turn 45 years old," it's time to reflect on the valuable insights and strategies you've gained for setting your children on a path to financial independence. In this concluding chapter, we will summarize the key takeaways from this book and encourage you to take action by implementing How to enable your children to become financially independent before they turn 45 years old in your family's financial journey.

Summarizing Key Takeaways

Throughout this book, we've explored a comprehensive blueprint for equipping your children with the knowledge and skills they need to achieve financial independence. Here are the key takeaways, elaborated in greater detail:

1. **Understanding Money:** Money plays a pivotal role in our lives, impacting our choices, opportunities, and future. Teaching your children about the value of money and how it works is the first step toward financial literacy.

Money is a fundamental aspect of modern life, influencing the decisions we make and the paths we pursue. It's crucial to instill in your children an early understanding of money's significance and the role it plays in achieving their life goals. By doing so, you empower them with the foundational knowledge they need to navigate the complex financial landscape.

2. **The Priority of Allocating Money for Assets:** Before your children can become financially independent, they must grasp the concept of allocating money for assets before liabilities. This means prioritizing investments that can grow over time.

Asset allocation is a fundamental principle in the journey to financial independence. It's not just about accumulating money; it's about making strategic decisions that enable your children's wealth to grow consistently. This concept teaches them that responsible financial management involves prioritizing investments and wealth-building over unnecessary expenses.

3. **The Power of Compounding:** Compound interest is a force that can exponentially increase wealth over the long term. By teaching your children how compounding works and the benefits of asset allocation, you set them on a path to financial growth.

Compound interest is a magical phenomenon that can turn modest savings into substantial wealth over time. By explaining the mechanics of compounding to your children, you empower them with the knowledge of how their money can work for them, making their financial dreams more attainable.

4. **Your Role as a Financial Mentor:** As a parent, you have a critical role in your children's financial education. It's your responsibility to teach asset allocation and financial principles, providing them with a strong foundation for their financial future.

Parental guidance is the cornerstone of effective financial education. By taking an active role in teaching your children about asset allocation and financial principles, you become their trusted mentor on their journey to financial independence. Your guidance and support are invaluable in shaping their financial mindset.

5. **Building a Strong Financial Foundation:** Budgeting, saving, and wisely allocating income to savings and investments are essential skills for financial stability. Help your children develop these habits from an early age.

Building a strong financial foundation begins with teaching your children the fundamental skills of budgeting, saving, and responsible financial management. These skills not only foster financial stability but also create a sense of control and empowerment over their financial futures.

6. **Value Investing Demystified:** Introduce your children to the principles of value investing, emphasizing the importance of a disciplined, long-term approach to building wealth.

Value investing is a time-tested strategy that can lead to sustainable wealth creation. By demystifying this approach and highlighting its principles to your children, you equip them with a proven strategy for making informed investment decisions. Value investing emphasizes discipline, patience, and a focus on long-term growth, qualities that are essential for financial success.

7. **How to enable your children to become financially independent before they turn 45 years old:** Setting up investment accounts for your children and teaching them about asset allocation within these accounts is a crucial step in their financial journey.

How to enable your children to become financially independent before they turn 45 years old serves as a structured framework for building wealth systematically. By establishing investment accounts for your children and teaching them the art of asset allocation within these accounts, you provide them with a tangible plan for wealth accumulation. This blueprint ensures that their financial resources are strategically deployed to achieve their financial goals.

8. **Creating a Wealth Growth Strategy:** Develop a long-term investment strategy that aligns with your children's financial goals. Use real-life case studies of successful asset allocators to inspire and guide their approach.

Crafting a wealth growth strategy is a deliberate and thoughtful process. It involves defining clear financial goals, assessing risk tolerance, and selecting appropriate asset allocations. Real-life case studies of successful asset allocators offer valuable insights and inspiration, showcasing how strategic planning and disciplined execution can lead to financial success.

9. **Teaching Financial Discipline:** Instill good financial habits in your children, emphasizing discipline in allocating funds to assets and making responsible financial decisions.

Financial discipline is a cornerstone of financial independence. It involves developing habits that prioritize long-term financial goals over short-term impulses. Teaching your children the importance of disciplined financial behavior, including consistent asset allocation, lays the groundwork for their financial well-being.

10. **Passing on the Knowledge:** Recognize the importance of financial education and provide age-appropriate financial lessons to your children.

Financial education is an ongoing process that evolves as your children grow and mature. It involves tailoring lessons and concepts to their age and level of understanding. By consistently offering age-appropriate financial education, you empower your children to make informed financial decisions at every stage of their lives.

11. **Monitoring and Adjusting:** Continuously track and manage the investment portfolio, adjusting asset allocation as needed to achieve long-term financial goals.

Successful asset allocation is not a static process; it requires ongoing monitoring and adjustment. By teaching your children to regularly assess their investment portfolios and make informed decisions based on changing circumstances, you instill a dynamic and adaptive approach to wealth management.

12. **Overcoming Challenges:** Understand common setbacks and develop strategies to address them, all while maintaining a steadfast commitment to asset allocation.

Challenges are an inherent part of the financial journey. By preparing your children to navigate common setbacks, such as market volatility or unexpected expenses, you equip them with resilience and the ability to stay committed to their asset allocation strategy, regardless of external circumstances.

13. **Preparing for the Future:** Equip your children with financial responsibility through early education, responsible asset management, and inheritance planning that reflects your values.

Preparing your children for the future involves a holistic approach that encompasses early financial education, responsible asset management, and thoughtful inheritance planning. By combining these elements, you ensure that your children are well-prepared to manage their financial affairs and continue the legacy of responsible wealth management.

Encouraging Implementation of How to enable your children to become financially independent before they turn 45 years old

Now that you have a comprehensive understanding of how to prepare your children for financial independence, it's time to take action. Implementing How to enable your children to become financially independent before they turn 45 years old is a transformative journey that requires commitment, dedication, and a steadfast belief in the power of financial education. Here are steps to help you implement this blueprint effectively:

1. **Start Early:** Begin teaching your children about money and financial principles from a young age. Use age-appropriate methods to make learning enjoyable and relatable. Incorporate financial discussions into everyday life and encourage your children to ask questions and explore financial concepts.

Early exposure to financial concepts sets the stage for a lifetime of financial literacy. Take advantage of teachable moments in daily life to reinforce key lessons. For example, involve your children in grocery shopping, explaining price comparisons and budgeting choices as you go.

2. **Engage in Open Communication:** Foster a culture of open communication about money within your family. Encourage questions, discussions, and financial decision-making involving your children. Create a safe and non-judgmental space where your children feel

comfortable sharing their financial thoughts and concerns.

Effective communication is the foundation of successful financial education. Make it a habit to have regular family discussions about money matters. These discussions can cover a wide range of topics, from setting financial goals to exploring investment options and even making charitable giving decisions as a family.

3. **Lead by Example:** Demonstrate responsible financial habits in your daily life. Your actions and values will serve as powerful lessons for your children. Model the behaviors and attitudes you wish to instill in them, showing the practical application of financial principles.

Children learn by observing the adults in their lives. Your financial decisions and behaviors are influential role models. Be mindful of the financial choices you make and how you explain them to your children. Share stories of your financial successes and challenges to provide real-world context.

4. **Set Clear Goals:** Help your children set financial goals and guide them in creating plans to achieve these objectives. Celebrate their successes along the way. Setting goals and celebrating milestones are effective ways to keep your children motivated and engaged in their financial journey.

Goal setting is a powerful tool for teaching your children the importance of planning and discipline. Encourage them to identify both short-term and long-term financial goals. Whether it's saving for a specific toy, a family vacation, or their college education, these goals become tangible motivators for responsible financial behavior.

5. **Utilize Resources:** Invest in financial education resources and professionals who can assist in your children's financial journey. Consider enrolling them in courses or programs designed to enhance their financial literacy. Seek out books, online resources, and workshops tailored to children and teenagers.

The wealth of financial education resources available today makes it easier than ever to support your children's learning. Explore age-appropriate books and interactive online tools that make financial concepts accessible and engaging. Consider enrolling your children in financial literacy programs or camps that provide hands-on learning experiences.

6. **Monitor and Adjust:** Continuously monitor your children's progress in their financial education and asset allocation strategies. Adjust and refine their plans as they grow and circumstances change. Regularly reviewing their financial goals and portfolio performance ensures that their strategies remain aligned with their evolving needs and aspirations.

Just as you track your own financial progress, encourage your children to regularly assess their financial goals and investment portfolios. Teach them how to evaluate their financial performance, identify areas for improvement, and make informed adjustments. This practice instills a proactive approach to financial management.

7. **Emphasize Long-Term Thinking:** Instill the importance of a long-term perspective in financial decision-making. Teach your children to resist impulsive choices and stay committed to their financial goals, even when faced with short-term temptations.

Patience and long-term thinking are virtues that underpin successful financial independence. Share stories of individuals who achieved their financial dreams through consistent, disciplined, and patient investment practices. Emphasize the value of delayed gratification and the rewards it can bring.

8. **Plan for the Future:** Develop a comprehensive estate plan that aligns with your values and financial goals. Communicate your intentions and expectations regarding wealth management and inheritance to your heirs. Engage legal and financial professionals to ensure that your estate plan is legally sound and in accordance with your wishes.

Estate planning is a critical component of your family's financial legacy. Work closely with professionals who specialize in estate law and financial planning to create a plan that addresses your specific goals and circumstances. Regularly review and update your estate plan to account for changes in your family's needs and financial situation.

By putting these principles into practice and following the steps outlined above, you'll be taking significant steps toward setting your children on a path to financial independence and ensuring the enduring prosperity of your family's wealth.

In Closing

In closing, remember that financial independence is not solely about the accumulation of wealth but also about the knowledge, discipline, and values that empower individuals to make informed financial decisions. By imparting these essential skills and principles to your children, you are providing them with a lasting legacy that transcends generations.

The journey to financial independence is a lifelong endeavor, and it begins with the foundation you lay for your children today. Your commitment to their financial education and responsible asset allocation will equip them with the tools they need to navigate a complex and ever-changing financial landscape.

We wish you and your family continued success on your journey towards financial independence. May the principles outlined in "How to enable your children to become financially independent before they turn 45 years old" serve as a guiding light, illuminating the path to financial empowerment for generations to come.

Appendices

In your quest for financial education and preparing your children for financial independence, it's paramount to have access to an extensive array of resources that can significantly enrich their learning experiences and amplify your teaching efforts. The appendices in this section aim to offer a comprehensive compendium of resources that span various facets of financial education and wealth management. These resources encompass books, websites, online courses, applications (apps), and tools meticulously curated to empower individuals of all ages with an expansive reservoir of financial knowledge and an arsenal of critical financial skills.

Appendix A: Recommended Books

Delve into a treasure trove of knowledge and insights with this meticulously selected list of recommended books. Each of these titles encapsulates unique perspectives on financial wisdom, asset management, and wealth creation.

1. **"Stock-Owl's Insight: Uncovering Value in the Stock Market"** My book on how to identify and analyze attractive stocks based on fundamental analysis.

2. **"Stock-Owl's Guide to Technical Mastery: Unveiling the Art of Stock Analysis"** My book on technical analysis and how to apply it in the stock market.

3. **"Rich Dad Poor Dad" by Robert Kiyosaki:** This seminal work dissects the contrast between financial philosophies and provides valuable lessons on financial literacy.

4. **"The Millionaire Next Door" by Thomas J. Stanley and William D. Danko:** An illuminating exploration of the habits and lifestyles of millionaires, replete with actionable wealth-building strategies.

5. **"The Richest Man in Babylon" by George S. Clason:** Set against the backdrop of ancient Babylon, this book imparts timeless financial principles through engaging stories and parables.

6. **"The Teenager's Guide to Money" by Joshua Holmberg and Joline Godfrey:** Tailored specifically for teenagers, this book offers a comprehensive approach to financial concepts, encompassing budgeting, saving, and investing.

7. **"The Simple Path to Wealth" by JL Collins:** Uncover a straightforward approach to achieving financial independence and early retirement, aligned with the "FIRE" movement (Financial Independence, Retire Early).

8. **"The Total Money Makeover" by Dave Ramsey:** A step-by-step guide to transforming your financial life, replete with practical tips and strategies.

9. **"The Bogleheads' Guide to Investing" by Taylor Larimore, Mel Lindauer, and Michael LeBoeuf:** A comprehensive resource for those seeking to understand and excel in the world of investing.

10. **"The Little Book of Common Sense Investing" by John C. Bogle:** Explore the principles of low-cost, index fund investing, a strategy championed by the founder of Vanguard.

11. **"I Will Teach You to Be Rich" by Ramit Sethi:** A practical guide to automating your finances and achieving financial success.

12. **"Your Money or Your Life" by Vicki Robin and Joe Dominguez:** This classic work delves into

the transformative power of understanding the relationship between money and life.

These recommended books collectively serve as a diverse library of financial wisdom, enabling you to explore varying perspectives and strategies for financial success.

Appendix B: Educational Websites

Embark on a digital journey of financial enlightenment by exploring an extensive list of educational websites, each offering a wealth of resources, articles, tutorials, and interactive content spanning a wide spectrum of financial topics.

1. **Stock-Owl** (www.stock-owl.com): My website with all of my insights into combining Fundamental and Technical Analysis to identify, enter and exit profitable trades in the stock market.

2. **Investopedia (**www.investopedia.com**):** A comprehensive online resource featuring a vast repository of articles, tutorials, and educational content that covers an expansive array of financial topics.

3. **Khan Academy (**www.khanacademy.org**):** Khan Academy offers free online courses in finance and economics suitable for learners of all ages, including specialized content tailored for kids and teenagers.

4. **MyMoney.gov (**www.mymoney.gov**):** A U.S. government website that equips you with tools and resources for personal financial planning, including budgeting and savings guidance.

5. **Practical Money Skills** (www.practicalmoneyskills.com**):** Developed by Visa, this website offers interactive financial

games, lesson plans, and resources designed for educators, parents, and students alike.

6. **Smart About Money** (www.smartaboutmoney.org): This website provides a comprehensive suite of financial courses, tools, and resources, empowering individuals to make informed financial decisions.

7. **The Balance** (www.thebalance.com): A trusted source of financial information, The Balance offers a wide range of articles and guides on topics spanning personal finance, investing, and retirement planning.

8. **Financial Industry Regulatory Authority (FINRA)** (www.finra.org): FINRA's website features educational content on investing, saving, and avoiding scams, along with tools and resources for financial decision-making.

9. **National Endowment for Financial Education (NEFE)** (www.nefe.org): NEFE provides an array of resources, including articles, guides, and tools, to enhance financial literacy and decision-making.

10. **Wise Bread** (www.wisebread.com): A personal finance website that offers a treasure trove of articles and tips on frugal living, saving money, and financial planning.

11. **Money Crashers (**www.moneycrashers.com**):** Explore articles and guides on personal finance, investing, and frugal living, along with resources for making informed financial choices.

These educational websites collectively form a robust digital ecosystem of financial knowledge, ensuring that you have access to a plethora of resources to bolster your financial understanding.

Appendix C: Online Courses and Programs

Elevate your financial acumen with an expansive selection of online courses and programs, carefully curated to cater to diverse learning preferences and objectives. These courses span a wide spectrum of financial topics, delivered by reputable institutions and organizations.

1. **Coursera (**www.coursera.org**):** Coursera offers a diverse array of online courses related to finance and economics, including options from renowned universities and institutions worldwide.

2. **edX (**www.edx.org**):** Explore courses from top universities and institutions worldwide, with numerous offerings related to finance, investing, and wealth management.

3. **Junior Achievement (**www.juniorachievement.org**):** Junior Achievement provides a variety of programs and resources designed to teach young people about financial literacy, entrepreneurship, and work-readiness.

4. **MIT OpenCourseWare (ocw.mit.edu):** Access a treasure trove of free course materials from the Massachusetts Institute of Technology (MIT), covering various finance-related subjects.

5. **Yale Online Courses (online-learning.yale.edu):** Yale University offers a

selection of online courses covering topics such as financial markets, economics, and personal finance.

6. **The Khan Academy Finance and Capital Markets Course** (www.khanacademy.org/college-careers-more/personal-finance): Dive into a comprehensive course that covers personal finance, investing, and capital markets, presented in an engaging format.

7. **Financial Planning Association (FPA) Learning Center** (www.financialplanningassociation.org/learning-center): Access a range of resources and courses focused on financial planning and wealth management.

8. **National Endowment for Financial Education (NEFE) High School Financial Planning Program** (www.hsfpp.org): NEFE offers a structured program designed to enhance financial literacy among high school students.

9. **Smart About Money Online Courses** (www.smartaboutmoney.org/Online-Courses): Explore a series of online courses that cover various financial topics, from budgeting to investing.

10. **Practical Money Skills Online Learning Center** (www.practicalmoneyskills.com/learn):

Discover a comprehensive online learning center offering courses on personal finance, budgeting, and more.

These online courses and programs provide a diverse range of learning opportunities, catering to learners of all levels and interests, whether you're seeking to strengthen your financial knowledge or provide valuable learning experiences for your children.

Appendix D: Financial Planning Tools and Apps

Navigate the complex world of financial management with a suite of financial planning tools and applications (apps) that can simplify budgeting, tracking expenses, and managing investments. These tools have been meticulously selected to accommodate various financial needs and preferences.

1. **Mint** (www.mint.com): A popular personal finance app that helps users create budgets, track expenses, and set financial goals, all in one place.

2. **Yodlee** (www.yodlee.com): A financial data aggregation and analytics platform that offers a comprehensive view of your financial accounts and transactions, facilitating holistic financial management.

3. **Personal Capital** (www.personalcapital.com): An all-in-one financial planning tool that combines budgeting, investment tracking, and retirement planning into a single platform.

4. **YNAB (You Need a Budget)** (www.youneedabudget.com): This app focuses on zero-based budgeting, helping users allocate every dollar to specific budget categories and achieve financial goals.

5. **Quicken** (www.quicken.com): A longstanding and comprehensive personal finance software

that enables detailed budgeting, investment tracking, and financial planning.

6. **MoneyWiz** (www.moneywizapp.com): A versatile personal finance app that offers budgeting, expense tracking, and investment management features, along with powerful reporting tools.

7. **Acorns** (www.acorns.com): An app that rounds up everyday purchases to the nearest dollar and invests the spare change, providing a simple way to start investing.

8. **Robinhood** (www.robinhood.com): A commission-free stock and cryptocurrency trading app that offers an accessible platform for beginners interested in investing.

9. **Morningstar** (www.morningstar.com): A comprehensive investment research platform that provides analysis, portfolio management, and financial planning resources.

10. **Google Sheets and Excel:** Leverage these spreadsheet applications to create custom budgeting and financial planning templates tailored to your specific needs and preferences.

These financial planning tools and apps cater to a wide range of financial management requirements, ensuring that you can select the ones that best align with your financial goals and preferences.

These expanded appendices collectively form an extensive and invaluable resource library, equipping you with a vast array of options for deepening your financial knowledge and skills. Whether you are on a personal journey of financial enlightenment or seeking to provide enriching learning opportunities for your children, these resources encompass books, websites, online courses, apps, and tools that can guide you on your path toward financial literacy and independence.

Appendix E: Glossary of Financial Terms

Navigating the world of finance can often feel like delving into a complex language with its own vocabulary. To facilitate your journey in comprehending the intricate terminology and jargon, this comprehensive glossary provides detailed, clear, and concise explanations of key financial terms and concepts. Whether you're just beginning your financial education or you're a seasoned investor, having access to this extensive glossary will empower you to engage confidently in financial discussions and make well-informed decisions.

In this glossary, you'll find an expansive range of terms, including but not limited to:

1. **Asset Allocation:** The strategic distribution of investments among various asset classes, such as stocks, bonds, real estate, and cash equivalents, with the goal of achieving specific financial objectives while managing risk. Effective asset allocation is a cornerstone of successful wealth management.

2. **Compound Interest:** A fundamental financial concept wherein interest is earned not only on the initial principal but also on the accumulated interest from prior periods. This phenomenon results in exponential growth of an investment over time, making it a powerful force for wealth accumulation.

3. **Diversification:** A risk management strategy involving the spread of investments across different assets or asset classes to mitigate risk. Diversification aims to avoid overconcentration in a single investment, reducing the impact of poor performance in any one area.

4. **Net Worth:** A critical financial metric that provides a snapshot of an individual's or a family's financial health. It is calculated as the total value of assets (what one owns) minus liabilities (what one owes). A positive net worth indicates financial well-being, while a negative net worth signals potential financial challenges.

5. **Risk Tolerance:** An individual's capacity and willingness to endure fluctuations in the value of their investments without making impulsive decisions. Understanding one's risk tolerance is crucial for creating a well-balanced and emotionally sustainable investment strategy.

6. **Liquidity:** The ease with which an asset or investment can be converted into cash without significant loss of value. Assets like cash and highly liquid securities are considered highly liquid, while real estate or certain investments may have lower liquidity.

7. **401(k):** A popular retirement savings plan in the United States that allows employees to contribute a portion of their salary to a tax-advantaged investment account. Employers may

also provide matching contributions, making 401(k)s a valuable retirement planning tool.

8. **Bull Market:** A market characterized by rising asset prices, optimism, and a positive investor sentiment. Bull markets often coincide with periods of strong economic growth and increasing corporate profits.

9. **Bear Market:** A market characterized by declining asset prices, pessimism, and a negative investor sentiment. Bear markets can be challenging for investors and may signal economic slowdowns or recessions.

10. **Credit Score:** A numerical representation of an individual's creditworthiness, used by lenders to assess the risk of extending credit. Credit scores are influenced by factors such as payment history, debt levels, and the length of credit history.

This expanded glossary aims to be your trusted companion in demystifying financial terminology, ensuring that you have access to comprehensive explanations that enhance your financial literacy and facilitate your ability to navigate the complex world of finance.

Appendix F: Worksheets and Templates

Practicality is the bedrock of effective financial planning. In this section, you will discover an extensive collection of meticulously crafted worksheets and templates designed to streamline your financial decision-making and planning processes. From budgeting templates to investment portfolio trackers, these versatile tools are here to simplify even the most intricate financial tasks and enable you to maintain impeccable organization on your path to financial independence.

Here's an overview of some of the worksheets and templates you'll find:

1. **Personal Budget Worksheet:** A comprehensive tool that empowers you to create, manage, and fine-tune your monthly budget. Track expenses, set financial goals, and gain a clear understanding of where your money is going.

2. **Asset Allocation Calculator:** An interactive and sophisticated calculator that assists you in determining the optimal distribution of your investments across various asset classes based on your specific financial goals and risk tolerance.

3. **Retirement Planning Template:** An in-depth template that enables you to estimate your retirement needs, set savings targets, and craft a detailed roadmap for your retirement years. It

takes into account factors like inflation, expected expenses, and investment returns.

4. **Debt Repayment Plan:** A meticulously structured plan designed to help you tackle and manage your debt efficiently. It includes strategies for paying down loans, managing interest rates, and becoming debt-free faster.

5. **Investment Portfolio Tracker:** An advanced Excel spreadsheet that provides comprehensive tools for monitoring the performance of your investments. This includes stocks, bonds, mutual funds, ETFs, and more. You can track historical performance, dividends, and analyze asset allocation.

6. **Financial Goal Setting Worksheet:** An insightful tool that guides you through the process of defining your financial objectives, prioritizing them based on importance, and developing actionable plans to achieve each goal. It ensures that you remain focused and committed to your financial aspirations.

7. **Savings Goal Tracker:** A flexible template that allows you to monitor your progress toward various savings goals, whether it's an emergency fund, a dream vacation, a down payment on a home, or other significant financial milestones.

8. **Expense Tracking Sheet:** A straightforward yet effective sheet for recording daily expenses,

categorizing them, and identifying areas where you can cut costs. It serves as a powerful tool for gaining control over your spending habits.

These worksheets and templates transcend mere financial tools; they are your companions on the journey to financial mastery. Whether you're crafting a meticulous budget, fine-tuning your asset allocation strategy, or meticulously tracking your investment portfolio, these practical tools are designed to simplify complex financial tasks and elevate your financial organization to new heights.

Acknowledgments

The journey towards financial independence and the mission to equip the next generation with financial acumen are endeavors deeply enriched by the support, wisdom, and encouragement of a community of remarkable individuals. As we navigate the intricate landscape of finance, it is with immense gratitude that we acknowledge and express our profound appreciation to those who have played pivotal roles in shaping our financial knowledge and aspirations.

I extend our heartfelt appreciation to:

1. **Family:** Our gratitude knows no bounds as we recognize the foundational role our parents have played in instilling within us the values of financial responsibility and diligence from the very beginning. My amazing wife, our three children, our inspiration and motivation, who propel us to build a sturdy financial framework for their future.

2. **Mentors:** It is with deep respect and gratitude that we acknowledge the mentors and educators who generously shared their wealth of financial expertise and wisdom. Their guidance has been instrumental in steering me toward sound financial practices and effective investment strategies.

3. **Readers:** To my esteemed readers, I extend my gratitude for joining me on this profound

journey. Your unwavering commitment to financial education and the pursuit of independence is the driving force behind the creation of this book.

4. **Financial Community:** My heartfelt appreciation goes out to the vibrant community of financial professionals, bloggers, and enthusiasts who tirelessly share their insights and experiences. Your contributions enrich the collective understanding of finance, creating a more informed and empowered society.

5. **Colleagues and Friends:** I am grateful beyond measure to our colleagues and friends who have provided steadfast support, unwavering encouragement, and countless insightful conversations throughout the arduous yet rewarding process of crafting this book.

6. **Authors and Thought Leaders:** I acknowledge and express my appreciation to the authors and thought leaders in the field of finance and wealth management. Their pioneering works have blazed the trail for financial literacy and independence, laying the foundation upon which we build.

7. **Life's Lessons:** Every experience, whether triumphant or challenging, holds immeasurable value in shaping our financial journeys. I express my gratitude to the myriad lessons life has

presented, underscoring the significance of financial wisdom and resilience.

8. **The Future:** My dedication and commitment extend to the future generations. It is my privilege to nurture and safeguard the financial independence and prosperity of those who will follow in our footsteps.

Your unwavering support, guidance, and enthusiasm have been instrumental in the creation of this book and the pursuit of our shared mission. Together, we are building a legacy of financial empowerment that will resonate across generations, ensuring a brighter and more financially secure future for all.

Index

Welcome to the extensive quick reference guide, a meticulously curated resource designed to provide you with effortless access to a vast array of key concepts, topics, and subtopics meticulously explored within this book. Whether you are seeking comprehensive explanations, in-depth insights, or swift navigation to specific areas of interest, this meticulously crafted index stands as your invaluable navigator for swiftly locating the precise information you seek.

Please utilize this enriched index to access a multitude of key topics and subtopics:

- **Exploring Compound Interest:**

    - The Mechanism of Compound Interest

    - Time as a Catalyst for Compound Interest

    - Compounding Frequencies: Monthly, Quarterly, and More

- **Maximizing Growth through Compound Interest:**

    - Compound Interest in Investment Vehicles

    - Compound Interest in Savings Accounts

    - Compound Interest Strategies for Financial Success

D - Diversification

- **Understanding Diversification:**

    - Principles of Diversification

    - Types of Asset Classes for Diversification

    - The Art of Portfolio Diversification

- **Benefits of Diversification:**

    - Risk Reduction Through Diversification

    - Diversification and Volatile Markets

    - Historical Case Studies of Successful Diversification

F - Financial Independence

- **The Journey to Financial Independence:**
    - Paths to Financial Independence
    - The Psychology of Financial Independence
    - Financial Independence and Quality of Life
- **Strategies for Achieving Financial Independence:**
    - Building Multiple Income Streams
    - Passive Income Strategies
    - Achieving Financial Independence through Investments

I - Investment Accounts

- **Setting Up Investment Accounts:**
    - Types of Investment Accounts
    - Selecting the Right Investment Platform
    - Tax-Efficient Investment Account Strategies
- **Asset Allocation in Investment Accounts:**
    - Strategies for Allocating Assets
    - Investment Account Optimization

- Monitoring and Adjusting Asset Allocation

P - Parental Role

- **Parental Responsibility in Financial Education:**
  - Early Financial Lessons for Children
  - Age-Appropriate Financial Education
  - Teaching Financial Responsibility

- **Teaching Asset Allocation to Children:**
  - Making Asset Allocation Fun for Kids
  - Games and Activities for Financial Education
  - Financial Literacy in School Curricula

S - Savings and Budgeting

- **Building a Strong Financial Foundation:**
  - The Importance of Financial Planning
  - Emergency Funds and Financial Security
  - Strategies for Reducing Debt

- **Budgeting and Saving Techniques:**
  - Advanced Budgeting Strategies
  - Savings Plans for Major Life Goals
  - Managing Lifestyle Inflation

V - Value Investing

- **Introduction to Value Investing:**
    - The Philosophy of Value Investing
    - Key Principles of Value Investing
    - Value Investing Legends and Success Stories

- **Value Investing and Asset Allocation:**
    - Integrating Value Investing into Asset Allocation
    - Risk Management in Value Investing
    - Value Investing in Different Market Conditions

W - Wealth Growth

- **Creating a Wealth Growth Strategy:**
    - Developing a Long-Term Wealth Growth Plan
    - Building a Diverse Investment Portfolio
    - Sustainable Wealth Growth Strategies

- **Case Studies of Successful Asset Allocators:**
    - Real-Life Success Stories in Asset Allocation
    - Learning from Notable Wealth Builders

- Adapting Successful Strategies to Your Portfolio

Your journey to financial independence and the empowerment of future generations begins here. Utilize this enriched index as your comprehensive guide to explore, comprehend, and expertly apply the extensive array of key concepts and subtopics meticulously detailed in "How to enable your children to become financially independent before they turn 45 years old."

About the Author

Stock-Owl, the alias under which the author operates, is a seasoned economist and master of international business with a deep passion for value investing and Technical Analysis. With a career spanning many years in the global international business arena, Stock-Owl has amassed a wealth of knowledge and experience that serves as the foundation for the investment philosophy explored in this book.

Stock-Owl's journey in value investing and Technical Analysis began as a quest for financial independence and a desire to understand the intricacies of the stock market. Drawing from academic achievements and practical experiences in international business, Stock-Owl embarked on a personal exploration of the world of finance, armed with a determination to master the art of value investing matched with Technical Analysis.

Over the years, Stock-Owl honed its analytical skills, delving into the works of legendary value investors such as Benjamin Graham and Warren Buffett. This dedication to continuous learning and improvement led to the development of a unique approach to value investing — one that combines academic rigor with practical wisdom gained from years of navigating the complexities of global markets.

Stock-Owl's commitment to financial education and empowerment is evident not only in this book but also in their contributions to the broader financial community. Through the alias of Stock-Owl, the author has shared insights, analyses, and investment philosophies with a growing audience of like-minded investors and enthusiasts.

As an advocate for the principles of value investing, Stock-Owl's mission is to empower individuals to take control of their financial futures. Stock-Owl believes that by understanding the fundamentals of solid, fundamentally sound investments, individuals can achieve financial independence and make informed decisions to secure their financial well-being.

In this book, Stock-Owl shares its expertise, knowledge, and passion for value investing, offering readers a comprehensive guide to identifying and investing in solid stocks. Through the lens of Stock-Owl's alias, readers can embark on their own journeys of financial discovery, equipped with the tools and principles of value investing.

Join Stock-Owl on this exploration of value investing and investing matched with technical analysis, and discover the potential to unlock financial freedom and success in the world of stocks.

You can follow Stock-Owl online on www.stock-owl.com and www.x.com under "Stock-Owl".